"Marcelo got to the top, and he remains there because he constantly
I was in São Paulo, Brazil coaching at the 2003 ADCC World Cham
celo shocked the grappling world. I watched the "unknown" last m
unique method to outclass the world's finest and win the championship. He won the following ADCC in 2005, and again won the next ADCC in 2007. But this time he used an entirely new approach. This book is the current culmination of his amazing evolution, and gives you everything you need to be years ahead of the competition."

Burton Richardson, MMAForTheStreet.com

"I met Marcelo through my first black belt, Fabio Gurgel, who is also Marcelo's teacher. I had the pleasure to corner him for a competition in Ohio, which he won. After that, his career in the United States skyrocketed and he became the superstar he is now. Marcelo is a great guy, very funny, a heck of a fighter, and a great teacher. He is always smiling and willing to help his friends and students. Even with his fame, he is still the same kid from Formiga, his hometown in Minas Gerais, humble and attentive to all. He has made history in jiu-jitsu and in our team, Alliance, and he is a true representative of our teaching and fighting style."

Jacare Cavalcanti, Alliance Head Instructor

"Marcelo has developed a complete guard system that works both gi and no-gi on all body types. Using his four limbs on his opponent's two legs, he is able to execute highly effective sweeps and then lock in a submission. If you haven't studied the x-guard, you have a huge hole in your game."

Scott Nelson, Onthemat.com

"Marcelo Garcia is an inspiration for all of us who live with a hunger for quality. Anyone who knows grappling has admired his fluidity on the mats, his determination of spirit, his incredible courage and clarity of expression under fire. But perhaps what is most impressive about Marcelo is his relentless creativity. Garcia is a dynamic innovator at the cutting edge of the evolution of this beautiful art, and I for one can't wait to see what will come next."

Josh Waitzkin, author, The Art of Learning

RELATED BOOKS BY VICTORY BELT

Mastering the Rubber Guard by Eddie Bravo with Erich Krauss & Glen Cordoza

Mastering the Rubber Guard DVD by Eddie Bravo with the Victory Belt Staff

Guerrilla Jiu-Jitsu: Revolutionizing Brazilian Jiu-Jitsu by Dave Camarillo with Erich Krauss

Mixed Martial Arts: The Book of Knowledge by BJ Penn with Glen Cordoza & Erich Krauss

Wrestling for Fighting: The Natural Way by Randy Couture with Erich Krauss & Glen Cordoza

Mastering the Twister by Eddie Bravo with Erich Krauss & Glen Cordoza

COMING SOON BY VICTORY BELT

Judo for Fighting by Karo Parisyan with Erich Krauss & Glen Cordoza

FEDOR by Fedor Emelianenko with Erich Krauss & Glen Cordoza

MMA by Anderson Silva with Erich Krauss & Glen Cordoza

From Wrestling to MMA by Matt Lindland with Glen Cordoza & Erich Krauss

Minotauro by Antonio Rodrigo Nogueira with Erich Krauss & Glen Cordoza

Guerrilla Jiu-Jitsu for MMA by Dave Camarillo with Kevin Howell

Arm Drags and Back Attacks by Marcelo Garcia with Erich Krauss & Glen Cordoza

Ultimate Competition Jiu-Jitsu by Andre Galvao with Kevin Howell

Karate for Mixed Martial Arts by Lyoto Machida with Erich Krauss & Glen Cordoza

Jiu-Jitsu: The Universal Language by Saulo Ribeiro with Kevin Howell

In The Shark Tank by Kelly Crigger

THE X-GUARD
GI & NO-GI JIU-JITSU

MARCELO GARCIA
WITH GLEN CORDOZA & ERICH KRAUSS
PHOTOGRAPHY BY ERIC HENDRIKX

California

First Published in 2007 by Victory Belt Publishing.

Copyright © 2007 Marcelo Garcia, Erich Krauss & Glen Cordoza

All rights reserved. No part of this publication may be reproduced or distributed in any form or by any means, electronic or mechanical, or stored in a database or retrieval system, without prior written permission from the publisher.

ISBN 10: 0-9777315-0-2
ISBN 13: 9780977731503

This book is for educational purposes. The publisher and authors of this instructional book are not responsible in any manner whatsoever for any adverse effects arising directly or indirectly as a result of the information provided in this book. If not practiced safely and with caution, martial arts can be dangerous to you and to others. It is important to consult with a professional martial arts instructor before beginning training. It is also very important to consult with a physician prior to training due to the intense and strenuous nature of the techniques in this book.

Victory Belt ® is a registered trademark of Victory Belt Publishing.
Printed in Hong Kong
Cover Design by BRIAN RULE

CONTENTS

Acknowledgments 8
Introduction 9
The X-Guard 23

BUTTERFLY GUARD

BASIC POSITIONING & GRIP DEFENSE

Butterfly Guard Stance	28	GI / NO-GI
Hand Control	29	GI / NO-GI
Breaking Inside Pant Sleeve Grip	29	GI / NO-GI
Breaking Inside Leg Grip	30	GI / NO-GI
Breaking Outside Leg Grip	30	GI / NO-GI
Breaking Collar Grip	31	GI / NO-GI
Collar & Sleeve Control	32	GI / NO-GI
Collar Grip Variations	32	GI / NO-GI
Head & Arm Control	33	GI / NO-GI
Double Underhook Control	34	GI / NO-GI
Double Underhook Control (No-Gi Variation)	34	GI / NO-GI
Cross Arm Grip	35	GI / NO-GI
Cross Arm Grip to Arm Drag	36	GI / NO-GI

SWEEPS & TRANSITIONS

Collar & Sleeve Control Butterfly Sweep	38	GI / NO-GI
Head & Arm Control Butterfly Sweep	41	GI / NO-GI
Collar & Sleeve Control Butterfly Sweep 2	44	GI / NO-GI
Ankle Pick Butterfly Sweep	47	GI / NO-GI
Double Underhook Butterfly Sweep	50	GI / NO-GI
Double Underhook Butterfly Sweep (No-Gi)	53	GI / NO-GI
Double Underhook Push Back Sweep	56	GI / NO-GI
Half Butterfly Sweep (Off Pummel)	59	GI / NO-GI
Stomp Kick Half Butterfly Sweep (Off Pummel)	63	GI / NO-GI
Cross Arm Grip to Back Transition	67	GI / NO-GI
Arm Drag Reverse Sweep	70	GI / NO-GI
Cross Arm Control	75	GI / NO-GI
Cross Arm Control Underhook Sweep	77	GI / NO-GI
Cross Arm Control Half Butterfly Sweep 1	79	GI / NO-GI
Cross Arm Control Half Butterfly Sweep 2	82	GI / NO-GI
Cross Arm Control Reverse Sweep 1	85	GI / NO-GI
Cross Arm Control Reverse Sweep 2	88	GI / NO-GI

SUBMISSIONS

Straight Armbar	92	👍 GI / 👍 NO-GI
Triangle Armbar Finish	94	👍 GI / 👍 NO-GI
Triangle Finish	96	👍 GI / 👍 NO-GI
Omoplata	98	👍 GI / 👍 NO-GI
Monoplata	101	👍 GI / 👍 NO-GI
Guillotine Choke	104	👍 GI / 👍 NO-GI
Off Balance Guillotine Choke Sequence	106	👍 GI / 👍 NO-GI

THE X-GUARD

ESTABLISHING THE X-GUARD

Single Leg to X-Guard Setup	112	👍 GI / 👍 NO-GI
Pulling The X-Guard from Standing	115	👍 GI / 👎 NO-GI
Double Knee Control to X-Guard	119	👍 GI / 👍 NO-GI
Single Leg Attack From Bottom Position	122	👍 GI / 👍 NO-GI
Collar & Sleeve Control to X-Guard	125	👍 GI / 👎 NO-GI
Head & Wrist Control to X-Guard	128	👍 GI / 👍 NO-GI
Cross Grip Sleeve Control to X-Guard	132	👍 GI / 👎 NO-GI
Cross Grip to Arm Drag X-Guard Setup	137	👍 GI / 👍 NO-GI
Double Elbow Control to X-Guard	142	👍 GI / 👍 NO-GI
Double Underhook Control to X-Guard	146	👍 GI / 👍 NO-GI
Full Guard to X-Guard	150	👍 GI / 👎 NO-GI
Full Guard to X-Guard (Opponent Standing)	154	👍 GI / 👎 NO-GI
Full Guard to X-Guard (No-Gi/Opponent Standing)	158	👍 GI / 👍 NO-GI
Half Guard to X-Guard (Option 1)	162	👍 GI / 👍 NO-GI
Half Guard to X-Guard (Option 2)	166	👍 GI / 👍 NO-GI
Omoplata to X-Guard	170	👍 GI / 👍 NO-GI
Mount Escape to X-Guard	172	👍 GI / 👍 NO-GI
Front Headlock Escape to X-Guard	175	👍 GI / 👍 NO-GI

SWEEPS

Far Sleeve Control Sweep (Opponent Kneeling)	180	👍 GI / 👎 NO-GI
Far Wrist Control Sweep	183	👍 GI / 👍 NO-GI
Far Sleeve Control Sweep (Opponent Standing)	186	👍 GI / 👎 NO-GI
Near Sleeve Control Switch Sweep (Opponent Kneeling)	189	👍 GI / 👎 NO-GI
Near Wrist Control Switch Sweep	194	👍 GI / 👍 NO-GI
Near Sleeve Control Switch Sweep (Opponent Standing)	198	👍 GI / 👎 NO-GI
Near Sleeve & Armpit Control Sweep	201	👍 GI / 👎 NO-GI
Sleeve & Leg Control Takedown Sweep	204	👍 GI / 👎 NO-GI
Takedown Sweep	207	👍 GI / 👍 NO-GI

Sleeve & Leg Control Reverse Sweep (Opponent Kneeling)........................ 210	GI /	NO-GI
Sleeve & Leg Control Reverse Sweep (Opponent Standing)........................ 214	GI /	NO-GI
Sleeve & Leg Control Scissor Sweep 218	GI /	NO-GI
Sleeve & Leg Control Push Sweep 221	GI /	NO-GI
X-Guard Push Sweep 225	GI /	NO-GI
Sleeve & Leg Control Push Sweep Variation 228	GI /	NO-GI
X-Guard Push Sweep Variation 233	GI /	NO-GI
Sleeve & Leg Control Pull Back Sweep......................................237	GI /	NO-GI
X-Guard Pull Back Sweep...241	GI /	NO-GI

SUBMISSIONS

Omoplata 246	GI /	NO-GI
Triangle... 249	GI /	NO-GI
Inverted Armbar (Gi)... 252	GI /	NO-GI
Inverted Armbar (No-Gi) 254	GI /	NO-GI
Knee Bar.. 256	GI /	NO-GI
Foot Lock 259	GI /	NO-GI
Heel Hook...261	GI /	NO-GI

About the Authors.. 264

Acknowledgments

To my father, Marcio Vespucio,

my mother, Luzia Garcia,

my sister, Monica,

my brother, Pedro,

my brother in-law, Gerson,

my beautiful wife, Tatiana Tognini Garcia.

To all my teachers, Iran Brasileiro, Paulo Cesar Resende, and Fabio Gurgel. And to my good friend Rommel Leite, who always told me I was on the same level as the other guys.

INTRODUCTION

Mom, dad, and me.

As a child I'd hear about the unusual things taking place in the big cities like Rio De Janeiro and São Paulo, but growing up in the center of Brazil in the town of Formiga, which translates to the English world "ant," seldom did I get to experience them firsthand.

On any given evening, I pretty much knew what to expect out of my town. I could find the elderly men in the plaza, playing cards and chess. Those who had families to support would be working the various shops and factories. And a large percentage of the children my age would be out drinking and getting into trouble due to the lack of a beach or extracurricular activities.

Everyone in Formiga wore common clothes and partook in common activities. It was pretty much your run-of-the-mill small town where everyone fell into the few available grooves. The biggest thing to look forward to was the fiesta that followed around our local soccer team.

For some reason, I always wanted something different than what the town had to offer. Instead of looking in my backyard for interests to keep me busy, I looked toward the horizon. However, not much came over the horizon due to our positioning in the world, so I ended up looking to the television. From the get-go, martial arts movies like *The Karate Kid* were my absolute favorites. Jiu-jitsu was already tremendously popular in Rio, but few people had even heard of the sport in Formiga. As a result, I was under the assumption that karate was the most effective martial art on the planet. I didn't have a preference as to what type of karate—I just wanted to learn how to punch and kick like the legends on the silver screen.

Luckily, Formiga was large enough to have a karate school. I jumped in with both feet at the age of eight, working with great determination on my striking and kata, but after four years of this, I still didn't have a clear idea of exactly what I was supposed to learn. I knew all the punches and kicks, but I hadn't been taught when to employ those punches and kicks based upon my opponent's actions. I didn't know if I had some genetic flaw or if my instructor was shrouding key knowledge. Karate was the only thing I had cooking, and needless to say, I grew tremendously disappointed.

Between the age of twelve and thirteen I lost the spirit of the martial arts. The temptation to use drugs and alcohol like many of my peers grew strong, but I thought I would give martial arts one more shot when a karate friend of mine told me he was thinking about starting judo. Having been brainwashed by Bruce Lee movies, I didn't have high hopes for a martial art that involved grappling. If my opponent attempted to grab me, all I needed to do to fend him off was punch or kick him in the face. But not wanting to abandon the most important thing in my life without at least giving it a second chance, I gathered the courage to visit the judo dojo and watch class.

Viewing kids throw each other onto the mats didn't do much to erase my skepticism. Every time they went to grab ahold of each other, I envisioned the strikes I could use to fend them off. Regardless, I decided to come back the next day and give it a shot. After all, if it was as bad as I imagined, I could just give up.

As it turned out, attending the class was much worse than I had imagined. The instructor's name was Fabiano Desouza, and he stuck me with a student who wasn't very mindful about using proper technique. The first time I got thrown, I lost my grip and got slammed hard on the mat (kind of like what happened to me when I fought Ricco Rodriguez in Abu Dhabi). Never had I taken that kind of abuse in karate, and immediately I thought, "If every throw is going to be like this, no way am I coming back." But not liking the alternatives to training judo, I staggered back to the judo dojo the following day.

This time I got paired up with someone who was a lot smaller than me, which caused me to take a whole lot less abuse. It gave me a chance to really take a step back and look at the sport. After just a few throws, I could feel how technique and strength could help you achieve your goal, which was to throw your opponent and then hold him on the mat. I felt how certain moves could be applied to a specific scenario. In the four years I had trained karate, never once had I gotten a good feel for what I could do to my opponent and my opponent could do to me, and here in judo I experienced it on my second day. It was quite frustrating because at every turn my opponents had full control, which they used to shake me from side to side and throw me again and again, but at least I had an understanding for what was possible.

Despite being the worst in my group for the first month, I fell in love with judo. Fabiano only offered classes three times a week, and I would go crazy on the days off. I remember one afternoon I made a calendar of all the days that I would get to train each month, and then after class I would cross off that session with a big X. I'm not quite sure why I did that,

New Year at my in-laws' house in Sao Paulo.

but I guess it had something to do with my paranoia about missing a chance to work out.

I put everything I had into training, and after a month or so my instructor told me it was time to compete. I wasn't nervous in the days leading up to the event because I had competed on a regular basis in karate, but the moment my opponent put his hands on me, I lost it. He shook me back and forth extremely hard and I didn't even feel it. It wasn't until thirty seconds had passed that I realized what was going on. I forced myself into the game, struggled through a back-and-forth battle, and ended up pulling out the win. The entire experience was quite enjoyable, but afterwards I was absolutely exhausted. It made me second-guess whether or not competition was my cup of tea, but it didn't really matter. Fabiano told me that every holiday there would be another event just like this one.

Unable to argue with my trainer, I quickly came to terms with his decision. It wasn't until later that I learned the young adult category didn't have separate divisions for the various belt ranking, which meant that a white belt like me would at some point get paired up with a much more experienced opponent.

Driving forward, I became the state champion in my belt within three months, and the state champion in all belts within five months. Judo became my life, making my days off grueling to get through. I had known all along that my coach was famous among other judoka in the area because he traveled several times a week to the neighboring city of Devinopolis to train jiu-jitsu, but I had never understood the difference between the two sports. Wanting to follow in his footsteps, I decided to find out one afternoon and asked if I could tag along.

An hour and a half bus ride took us to the academy of Iran Brasileiro, a jiu-jitsu black belt under Rickson Gracie. Karate and judo had been day and night, but when I saw the jiu-jitsu practitioners on the mat, their art seemed very similar to what I had been doing in judo. Basically, latch on to your opponent with a firm grip and fight hard. Of course there was much more to

Me and my first jiu-jitsu instructor, Iran Brasileiro de Alvarenga.

it than that, but making that simple association made it much easier for me to climb onto the mats.

I traveled with Fabiano to train jiu-jitsu several times a week. As I slowly started to progress in the new sport, I decided to begin competing. It worked out perfectly because I was currently having a rough time competing in judo due to the few extra pounds I had gained, which cast me into the no-weight limit division. I was thirteen at the time, and I had no idea how to shed that additional kilo to get back to the normal weight division. As a result, I was always the lightest no-weight competitor at the tournaments. The entire matter would resolve itself when I turned fourteen because the weight divisions rose and I would once again have a home, so I figured I would compete in jiu-jitsu in the meantime.

Things got off to a rocky start. I entered my first jiu-jitsu tournament three months after I had started and lost my first match of the day. Although I still planned to go back to judo competition at the year's

INTRODUCTION 11

end, I saw no reason to half-ass my jiu-jitsu training if I planned to continue to enter tournaments. I began making the voyage to Devinopolis three times a week instead of two, which wasn't easy on my family. After school I would have to skip lunch in order to catch the bus to the gym, and for a while my parents thought I was crazy. How can a fourteen-year-old boy pass up on lunch? They couldn't understand why I would sit three hours on a bus just to go train. Things got even more inconvenient when Fabiano decided to stop making the trip eight months after I had begun. But I was a man with a plan and began making solo missions.

My judo coach had ingrained within me the importance of repetitions with each technique, and nothing changed with Iran. The problem was I didn't have very many techniques in my arsenal to repeat in the beginning. I remember the first time Iran showed me how to properly apply the triangle choke on an opponent in my guard. For the longest time I had been trying to lock in the choke using just my legs, and rarely did I have success due to the shortness of my limbs. But when Iran showed me how to move my hips in order to obtain the proper angle, it made all the difference.

From that moment out, I became obsessed with the triangle. I learned how to apply it from nearly every position, both from the top and bottom. For some time, I'm sure my training partners and opponents thought it was the only submission I knew. I was under the assumption that trying to master a whole bunch of techniques at once wouldn't get me very far. I figured a better approach would be to pick one technique and learn it inside and out.

Between Fabiano and Iran's academies, I got to train most days out of the week. Several of my fellow judo students had also made the trip to Devinopolis at one time or another, so we managed to keep our skills sharp by grappling before and after judo class.

Despite all the hours I put into training, I still wasn't thrilled with the progress I was making. Our state of Minas Gerais was very weak in jiu-jitsu due to its location, and my instructor made no attempt to better our games by taking us to competitions outside of our region. A part of it had to do with a lack of funds to cart us all several hundred miles away, but that didn't ease my mind any. I wanted to know if I had good jiu-jitsu or bad jiu-jitsu, and I knew the only way I would ever find out for sure was to go up against competitors who had been training all their lives in the big cities like Rio.

On a quest to become the best jiu-jitsu competitor I could be, I picked up everything I could on the sport, which wasn't much. Jiu-jitsu wasn't ultra-popular like it is now, and Brazil only had one magazine that came out each month. The magazine was easy to find in the big cities, but I wasn't from a big city. Some months the publication wouldn't arrive in Formiga, and I would lose my mind because I would have to wait another entire month. Every time I got my hands on one, I would examine it like a mad scientist. It wasn't like the publications today where they show step-by-step instructions of the various moves. All they had was a single snap shot of a competitor finishing his opponent with a certain submission. I would then have to try and figure out how he set up that submission and where to apply pressure. I spent a great many hours on this form of analysis.

Then one day a jiu-jitsu special appeared on the television, and immediately I popped a tape into the VCR. A jiu-jitsu coach talked a few minutes about the sport and then rolled for three minutes with an opponent to demonstrate a handful of submissions. I must have watched that tape a hundred times, and from it I learned that when an opponent passed your guard, you could put him right back in by spinning and facing him. It seemed so simple, and I grew frustrated that I hadn't thought of that before. At the time, all I did was the closed guard. With my opponent trapped between my legs, I tried to lock in armbars and such.

There was obviously a whole lot more to learn, and it reaffirmed the fact that in order for me to reach my goal of becoming a jiu-jitsu champion, I would have to diversify and train with other people and camps. I would have to enter as many tournaments as possible.

But with all the good jiu-jitsu schools being located so far away, I just didn't see how that was possible.

Not long after this realization, I began venturing away from home to train jiu-jitsu any chance I could. I learned that there was a school in Ribeirao Preto, a city in São Paulo where my parents frequently went on vacation, and I talked Fabiano into going with me. The instant I walked into the school, which turned out to be Gracie Barra, I was completely blown away. Gordo, a famous Brazilian Jiu-Jitsu practitioner, was on the mats doing stuff I had never imagined possible. Instead of playing closed guard, he was holding his opponent's sleeves and had his feet on his biceps. I went through a single class, gleaned all that I could, and then returned home and practiced it with insane determination, not knowing if my form was even correct.

Another time I heard about a school just three hours from my home that had a blue belt champion among its ranks. I begged everyone I knew with a driver's license to take me. When I finally found someone, I went and trained for a day and then came home. I would have left town every day to train in a new gym, but we didn't have the money for it. I was limited to traveling once every three months.

Practicing the few techniques I picked up here and there, I continued entering tournaments. A highlight came when I won our state championships in the blue belt division. It gave me a glimmer of hope that perhaps the random jiu-jitsu training sessions were paying off, but I knew that the real test would be the Mundials, which I had qualified for by winning state. I entered the competition optimistic, but things didn't pan out so well. In my first match, my opponent latched on to my collar from the standing position and pulled guard. Immediately I hopped over his legs to pass his guard, but as I did this, he latched on to my opposite collar with his other hand. I figured once I moved into side control I would defend against the choke, but by spinning around him I only cinched the choke in tighter. A few seconds later, I woke up on the mat with the referee standing over me.

This loss cemented the fact that I wasn't doing what was needed to be on top. Even if I didn't have what it took to be on top, I still had to try. I had to learn the true meaning of sacrifice to get where I wanted to be.

A short while later I was at a tournament in my state and a jiu-jitsu coach named Paulo Resende asked why I had never come to train at his academy, which was located in Pocos de Caldas, a city ten hours away. He had a ton of students, but I had to decline because the travel would be nearly impossible.

"You don't have to just come for a day," he said. "If you decide to move there, you can sleep in a bunk bed in the academy, and I will supply you with lunch and dinner. To pay your way, you can clean the mats and help out with teaching."

It was the opportunity I had been waiting for. I was only sixteen at the time, and I told him I would first have to get permission from my parents, which I attempted to do immediately after the tournament. But my folks were not nearly as excited. In Brazil, seldom do children leave their parents' home until they go to college. And if they don't go to college, they live with their parents until they get married. They got very upset at the prospect, but following their supportive nature, they sadly told me it would be fine as long as I finished out the school year. So, I went to school for two more months and then packed my bags. Every

Hanging out with one of my first jiu-jitsu coaches, Paulo Resende.

INTRODUCTION 13

one in my family was very sad to see me go, but at the same time they wished me the best at following my dreams. My brother Pedro, a young man my father had taken off the streets, even bought me a brand new gi. The majority of jiu-jitsu uniforms in Brazil at that time were made from cheap cloth, but he had purchased me one from heavy-duty fabric. It had cost him an entire month's wages.

Three separate bus rides and ten hours later, I arrived at my new home, which consisted of a large mat room, a small bedroom, and an office. I had come to learn the meaning of sacrifice, and that's exactly what Paulo taught me. The first class was at six in the morning, and I had to wake up well ahead of that in order to dry the mats that were wetted by the leaky ceiling. When the students arrived, we'd head outside and run up the nearly vertical incline of a nearby mountain, then come back down and begin training. I also went through the second training at 8 am, and the third training at 3 pm. For the first few months I opted out of the 7 pm training in order to attend school, but eventually I decided that in order to continue to advance, I had to dedicate all of my focus on jiu-jitsu.

Pretty soon I dropped out of school and trained four times a day. I gleaned what I could from my instructor, who was a brown belt at the time, but I quickly learned that it doesn't really matter where you train if you're putting in four sessions a day. You're going to get better. I also continued to purchase any jiu-jitsu magazines I could get my hands on and break down the techniques.

As far as jiu-jitsu went, the biggest problem I encountered when I got there had to do with the guard. Coming from a judo background, I was great at taking my opponent down and passing his guard. Although this was an aggressive way to play jiu-jitsu, I was lost when an opponent landed in my guard. In order to eliminate this weakness, all I did for a long period of time was play guard. After many months of this, I got really good. My opponent began to think that playing guard was all I knew, and they would pull me into their guard to avoid my attacks, which brought me back to my specialty of passing.

Paulo noticed the advancements I was making, and one day at a tournament he told me that in addition to competing in my weight division, I would also have to compete in the absolute division.

"But they don't have an absolute in the teen division," was my instant comeback.

"You are correct. That's why you're going to compete in the adult absolute division."

I was sixteen at the time, and needless to say, I was quite nervous. "But I've never done that before."

"It doesn't matter," he said. "When we come to that point, we'll take a look at the competitors. If they are too big, then you don't have to compete."

It eased my mind a little, but not entirely. I competed in my division and ended up winning. Shortly thereafter, they began calling my name to enter my first absolute division match. Immediately I began looking around for my coach so we could take a look at the competitors, but he was nowhere to be found. I wandered around in circles asking people where my coach was, and eventually a guy approached me.

"Are you Marcelo Garcia?"

"Yes, I am."

"Well, come on then."

"Wait! I need to find my coach."

"There is no time."

I did what the man said and stepped out onto the mat. Thankfully, the absolute division had been separated into two brackets: Everyone under 210 pounds, and everyone over 210 pounds. The winner of each category would then face each other in the finals. I was in the under-210-pound bracket, but my opponent was still a great deal larger than me. In addition to being concerned about the size difference, I was also concerned about the rules. Unlike in normal competition, you couldn't win by points. You had to submit your opponent, which was a great deal harder to accomplish.

When my coach failed to materialize at the beginning of the match, I carried on without him and ended up defeating my opponent. It gave my confidence a tremendous boost, but that confidence was knocked back down a notch when I saw my final opponent. He was a grown man who weighed more than three hundred pounds. It was the last match of the day, the entire mat was open, and everyone's eyes were upon us.

Sucking it up, we went at it and I managed to get his back fifteen minutes into the bout. He quickly rolled out of bounds to avoid the choke, and then he refused to start in the same position when they put us back on the mat. We went at it again, and at the forty-five-minute mark I got his back again. This time I secured the rear naked choke and forced him to tap.

After the bout, my coach reappeared, and I thanked him for what he had done. If I had to pinpoint the most important thing I gained from him during our time together, it would have to be confidence. From that moment out, I competed in the absolute division in every competition.

Back at the gym, I continued to clean the mats every morning. And on the days when Paulo didn't show up for class, I'd teach the newer students. There were only a couple of downsides to the arrangement. The first was that the bunk bed Paulo promised me never materialized. I ended up sleeping on an old judo mat on the floor, and after several months I developed horrible bedsores all over my body. The second downside was that mornings in this new town were typically around forty degrees, which is unusually cold in Brazil. And during the times of year when the sun came out early, Paulo would start the morning classes an hour earlier so that we had to train before first light. But it all worked out in the end. After making a few complaints, Paulo ended up buying me that bunk bed, and I got used to the cold temperature. His goal was to teach us what it took to become a champion, and he succeeded. All I did was eat, sleep, and train. Jiu-jitsu became the center of my world.

This was of course very difficult on my family. My parents were getting up there in years, and even though I called my mother every day, I could hear the sadness in her voice each time we talked. She wanted me to become a responsible adult and find an honest profession. It probably wouldn't have been so hard on her if I could have gone home every weekend, but with the bus ride being ten hours each way, I only would have been able to spend a few hours with her before I had to leave again.

Pretty much the only people I saw outside of training during this time of my life were at the competitions. I remember those in charge of a tournament held in Rio were going to kick me out because I didn't have the entrance fee money, and a girl named Tatiana, who was also working with the coordinators, came to my rescue and convinced them to let me compete. When I got to the event, I introduced myself and thanked her. As it turned out, she was also a very advanced purple belt at the time, and I invited her to come to my gym in Pocos de Caldas to train because we had a lot of light students who were on her same level. She told me it would be a great idea, but I had no idea if anything would come of it.

Still retaining the goal of going as far as I could with jiu-jitsu, I again set my sights on some of the larger competitions. In Brazil, those competitions are the Nationals, the Team Competition, and the Mundials. I had already competed in the Mundials back home and failed, so I decided to give the Team Competition a stab. We were a part of Alliance, which included many academies, and they held an internal trial to see who would represent our state in the Team Competition.

I trained hard in preparation and ended up winning the trials. A short while later our entire team went to the competition and we ended up taking first place. It increased my confidence even more, and I decided to give the Mundials another shot.

While training for the event, Tatiana took me up on my offer and came to our gym to train. Originally she planned to stay with a girlfriend, but when the girlfriend backed out due to family problems, she ended up staying at the house I was now renting with other people from the school. After hanging out and training together for twenty days, Tatiana and I started dating. She had come with the intentions of training for just one month, but we ended up getting an apartment together. We couldn't afford furniture, just a mattress and a television, but it didn't bother us in the slightest. Jiu-jitsu was the center of both of our worlds.

Living together worked out nicely because Tatiana was also going to compete in the Mundials, but in the female division. We trained together for the next couple of months, earned our spots by winning the trials, and then traveled to Rio for the big day. I had some tough battles, but at the end of the day I had defeated all of my five opponents and took first in my division. Tatiana took second place in hers. All in all, it was a pretty darn good day. After several years devoting all of my time and energy into the sport, I was finally starting to make some headway.

I just didn't feel as though I was making enough headway. For some time Tatiana had been urging me to move to a bigger school in São Paulo because I would have more advanced students and instructors to train with. At first I didn't like the idea because I had sponsors for just about everything in Pocos de Caldas. They paid for my rent, my trips, and my entrance fees for the competitions. I was also loyal to Paulo. But then one day about three years after I had moved from my home, I realized that as long as I stayed, I would not get the instruction I needed to compete at a high level of competition. Paulo was an excellent teacher and very supportive, but he just didn't have the knowledge to take me to the next level.

I was quite nervous about making the move, but then a well-known jiu-jitsu instructor named Terere offered me a job to come teach with Leo Vieira at his school in São Paulo. It was exactly what I needed—a way to make money and still continue to train. I agreed immediately.

It would have worked out great if his academy was full of students, but it wasn't. I was making around fifty dollars a month. The only place Tatiana and I could afford was miles and miles away from the academy, and every morning I would take a two-hour bus ride to get there. I could have hopped on the express bus, which would put me there in an hour, but it cost an extra dollar and then I wouldn't have any money for lunch. As a result, I headed out early in the morning, taught the first session of the day, and then hung out until the evening class so I wouldn't have to make the four-hour round-trip journey. To pay the bills, Tatiana taught English lessons, sometimes twelve hours a day. Thankfully, her parents also lived in São Paulo and offered to help out when they could.

I refused to give up, and six months later Fabio Gurgel offered me a job to come teach at his school. I switched over to his academy, and slowly started earning a better salary from teaching. Things got even better when I began making small purses for winning competitions. The first time that happened was when I was a brown belt. I won two hundred dollars, and immediately I went out and purchased my mother a washing machine, something she'd never had.

The money might have been tight, but my jiu-jitsu made leaps and bounds while training with Fabio. There was only one downside about his academy—it didn't have any air-conditioning. I've always enjoyed a little heat while training, but Fabio's school

Receiving my black belt from Fabio Gurgel.

My wife and me after my first Mundials as a black belt in 2004.

was downright blistering. It was summertime when I first got there, and if anyone attempted to train with a gi, they would most likely have died from heat stroke within an hour. As a result, everyone trained exclusively no-gi.

"How am I supposed to do this?" was my first thought. "I have no idea how to do this." I had only trained without a gi once before, and I hadn't been very successful. But due to the circumstance, I didn't have an option. I was forced to adapt.

Fabio helped me every step of the way, and after a year rolling without the gi, I began to feel very comfortable. Still desiring to compete whenever and however I could, I decided to take a stab at Abu Dhabi, the largest and most respected no-gi grappling tournament in the world, which was held in Rio. I went to the trials and did great until the final match. I was up against Daniel Moraes. Prior to the trials, I had asked the referee if I would get penalized if I pulled guard, and he said that I would not. But when I pulled guard in the match, they took a point away from me. The instant that happened, Moraes did nothing. Since he was one point ahead, he decided to stall his way to victory. The match was so boring that it wasn't included on the ADCC DVD, even though it was the finals.

I figured that placing second in the trials still gave me a decent chance at getting into Abu Dhabi, but because the Mundials was a sure thing, I only trained one time a week without the gi for the next couple of months. As the event drew close, I gained some more hope when they allowed the fighter who had placed third in the trials into the event. Since I had placed second, I was certain that I, too, would be admitted. But apparently that wasn't the case. The other competitor got admitted because he was already popular with the fans, and I was still a nobody. It made me quite frustrated, but still I continued to train and diet like they were going to let me in.

It wasn't until I checked the official bracket on the Internet the morning before the weigh-ins that I realized I hadn't been admitted. After months of strict dieting and hard training, it was a huge let down. Immediately I went out and stuffed as much junk food down my throat as humanly possible. I waddled into training later that day, feeling utterly sick to my stomach from all the sugar I had consumed.

Just before I left for the night, Fabio received a call from one of the event coordinators. He said that an American named Dennis Hallman hadn't shown up, and if he still wasn't there by the weigh-ins the following day, I would be allowed to compete. Panicking about my weight, I instantly went for a three-hour run. When I got back, I settled into the sauna.

The following day, feeling sick and drained, I headed to the weigh-ins to learn that Hallman still hadn't arrived. I stepped on the scale, made weight, and got my official ticket into Abu Dhabi. Overjoyed, I took a look at the bracket and realized that perhaps my excitement was a bit premature. Across from me were competitors like Renzo Gracie, who had been my idol for some time, and Vitor Shaolin Ribeiro, one of the most dangerous competitors at that time.

I was very curious how things would turn out because I had never competed in an international no-gi grappling tournament before. My first competitor was Kiuma Kunioku, an excellent grappler out of Japan. I attempted a couple of arm drags while we were on our feet, and when that didn't go anywhere, I dropped to my back with the intention of establishing the x-guard. He scrambled, and I ended up in his guard, which I

Shortly after I won the Brazilian Competition Medium Weight & Absolute in 2006.

quickly passed into side control. He scrambled and pulled me back into his guard. The referee eventually broke us apart because we scooted out of bounds, and we were placed back in the middle of the mat. The instant the ref restarted the action, Kunioku turned away from me in an attempt to escape, and I leapt over him and took his back. A short while later, I locked in the rear naked choke.

Beating such an experienced no-gi grappler gave me a boost of confidence, but then I found myself up against Renzo Gracie. Back when I had first begun training jiu-jitsu, I had taken a picture with him at Gracie Barra. I was just a blue belt at the time, and he was already a black belt. In the picture, he looked like this massive guy compared to me, and now here I was competing against him. Leading up to the fight I tried not to think about his stature, and when we engaged, I kept telling myself over and over that no matter what happened, I would continue to give it my all and score points.

I pushed it hard right out of the gates. I attempted an arm drag to get a single leg takedown, but failed to bring him down to the mat. When we eventually did hit the mat, I immediately went to the x-guard. I attempted to sweep him from my trademark position, but Renzo was saved by his incredible base and balance. Still on my butt with Renzo standing, he executed a beautiful cartwheel over the top of me in an attempt to pass my guard, but I spun and put him back between my legs. I continued to stay busy, going for a guillotine, an arm drag, and then pulling him right back into the x-guard using the single leg control to x-guard setup technique you'll find in the fourth section of this book. This time, I managed to sweep him over to his back. If it had been a Brazilian Jiu-Jitsu tournament we were in, I would have racked up a decent amount of points, but in Abu Dhabi they don't score points for the first ten minutes of the fifteen-minute bout. This meant that all my hard work amounted to nothing.

Still, I had promised myself to keep working. I passed his guard into side control at one minute and fifty seconds into the fight. Renzo fought desperately to put me back into his guard, but I managed to remain in side control for the next two minutes, dominating the match. I always work best when my opponent attempts to escape a bad position because it creates openings, but Renzo's movements gave me no submission opportunities. Without many options, I focused on maintaining my position.

Finally, three minutes and thirty seconds in, Renzo turned away from me. Immediately I secured my far hook, claiming his back shortly thereafter using over-under control. For the remainder of the match I used all my energy to hold on, waiting for Renzo to make a mistake that would allow me to put him away. Although he attempted every escape in the book, rolling, flipping, standing, and shaking, not once did he offer me a clear route to the finish. When there were only thirty seconds left on the clock, Renzo managed to escape. The bout came to a conclusion with him in my closed guard. It had been a very tough battle, but I ended up defeating him on points.

Still with one more match to go to make it to the finals, a friend of mine rubbed out my arms, which were completely gassed. It made me feel a little better, but I knew that once I started my next bout, I would get tired again. That was the last thing I needed against Shaolin, one of the top competitors on the circuit.

My idol Rickson Gracie and me.

Luckily, I got the arm drag, secured a deep hook, and took his back very quickly. Shaolin scrambled about the mat in an attempt to escape, but I managed to apply a rear naked choke. Refusing to tap out, the referee pulled me off when he realized Shaolin had passed out.

Although I still had another fight to go before I could win my division, I felt all the hard work was behind me. I had just defeated a living legend and one of the top competitors in my weight division. However, the final match didn't prove to be a cakewalk. I went up against Otto Olsen, an accomplished wrestler from Michigan. As we wrestled back and forth in the standing position, each of us trying to tie up with the other in a favorable way, I got poked in the eye twice. It frustrated me, and I went from an arm drag to single leg, trying to pull the x-guard, but Otto scrambled out and got back to his feet. Once again, we tied up, and I went to the arm drag to single leg. He sunk in a guillotine choke in an attempt to defend, but his positioning allowed me to sweep him over to his back. To his credit, he exploded back to his feet the instant he landed. The ref restarted us because we had gone out of bounds, him standing and me on my butt. I scooted toward him, chasing him, and eventually backed him toward the edge of the mat, forcing him to engage. Immediately I transitioned to the x-guard. Otto defended against my sweeps very well, but because he was focusing on avoiding sweeps, it allowed me to transition to the knee bar, which I show in the sixth section of this book.

Before I could lock in the submission, we rolled out of bounds again. We were restarted in the middle, but we weren't put back into the same position. I didn't mind a whole lot because I was able to sit up, sweep Otto to his back, and pass his guard into side control. To defend, he wrapped up my neck and desperately tried to pull me back into his guard. Eventually, he turned into me, allowing me to take his back and immediately apply the rear naked choke.

Winning my division was a huge moment for me. For many years I had put all my focus into Brazilian Jiu-Jitsu, and now I realized that I was also good at no-gi grappling, which meant I had an entirely different avenue I could take. For a guy who lives for the martial arts and competition, that's pretty big.

With the ten thousand dollar prize money I received, I went out and purchased a 2000 Ford Focus to replace the '84 Volkswagen my father had been driving around. Both of my parents were from the old school, and for so long they couldn't comprehend what I was trying to achieve. They understood that you work and get paid for it, but what I did didn't seem like work to them. They had always wanted me to go to college, graduate, and get a decent-paying job, but when I showed up at his house with his new car, he realized that although I wasn't a doctor or a lawyer, I was still a professional. It had hurt them to see me stretch everything to the limit for so many years, but now they understood what all that hard work was for. I could make a decent living in jiu-jitsu.

I had predicted things would get better after my win, but I never realized how much better. Before I had been a nobody in the jiu-jitsu world, struggling to get invited to matches because no fans knew my name. Now I was getting invited to competitions left and right, as well as asked to give seminars, and I started to make a considerably better living.

Since the beginning of my career I had always felt I needed to take any opportunity that presented itself, and so the first time I had the chance to leave the country to compete and teach jiu-jitsu, I took it. After all, if I had never traveled from my hometown to other cities to learn jiu-jitsu, I never would have gotten this far. The only difference in this case was that I happened to be traveling much farther away.

The only downside was that I began traveling so much that I rarely found time to train. Eventually, I made the decision to move to the United States. Not only would it put me close to the big jiu-jitsu competitions, it would also put me close to the MMA competitions, which I one day wanted to enter. Now, with my loving wife by my side, I spend all day training and teaching martial arts, something that provides a good life for my family and gives me immense happiness. It puts a smile on my face from morning until night.

Our babies.

CHRONOLOGY OF CAREER AND TITLES WON BY MARCELO GARCIA

1997 BLUE BELT AWARDED

- 1997 / May – Champion of Minas Gerais Jiu-Jitsu State Competition, Blue Belt – MG / Brazil
- 1998 / May – Champion of Minas Jiu-Jitsu State Competition, Blue Belt – MG / Brazil
- 1999 / April – Champion of Brazilian Jiu-Jitsu Competition by Team / Heavyweight – RJ / Brazil
- 1999 / June – Champion of São Paulo Jiu-Jitsu State Competition / Heavyweight – SP / Brazil
- 1999 / July – World Champion, Juvenile Category / Heavyweight – RJ / Brazil

August 1999: PURPLE BELT AWARDED

- 2000 / June – Champion of São Paulo State Competition / Middleweight – SP / Brazil
- 2000 / July – World Champion Adult / Middleweight – RJ / Brazil

August 2000: BROWN BELT AWARDED

- 2000 / October – Second Place at Brazilian Comp. / Middleweight / Second Place Brazilian Competition Absolute Division – RJ / Brazil
- 2001 / June – Champion of São Paulo Jiu-Jitsu State Competition / Middleweight – SP / Brazil
- 2001 / October – Third Place at the Brazilian Competition / Absolute Division – Third Place/Middleweight – RJ / Brazil
- 2002 / April – Champion of São Paulo Jiu-Jitsu State Competition / Middleweight – SP/ Brazil
- 2002 / April – Second place at Brazilian by Team Competition / Heavyweight – RJ/Brazil
- 2002 / July – Second place at the World Jiu-Jitsu Competition / Middleweight – RJ/Brazil

August 2002: BLACK BELT AWARDED

- 2002 / September – São Paulo State Champion / Middleweight and Open Weight – SP/Brazil
- 2002 / October – Third Place Absolute Weight at Brazilian Competition – RJ / Brazil
- 2003 / May – Champion of ADCC – Submission Grappling – up to 76 kg Category – Awarded Most Technical Fighter – SP / Brazil
- 2003 / June – Second Place Brazilian Competition by Team/Heavyweight – RJ/Brazil
- 2003 / July – Second Place at the World Jiu-Jitsu Competition – RJ/Brazil
- 2004 / March – 2005/ March – Champion of Arnold Schwarzenegger Submission Competition / Heavyweight / Columbus – Ohio / USA
- 2004 / May – Champion of Brazilian Competition Middleweight / Second place absolute division – RJ / Brazil
- 2004 / July – World Champion of Brazilian Jiu-Jitsu / Middleweight / Second Place Absolute Division – RJ / Brazil
- 2005 / March – Champion of Arnold Schwarzenegger Submission Competition / Heavyweight / Ohio – USA
- 2005 / May – Champion of ADCC – Submission Grappling – up to 76 kg Category – Awarded Best Fight – Long Beach / CA – USA
- 2005 / June – Champion of Coca Cola Submission Competition – Atlanta / GA – USA
- 2005 / November – Champion of Alliance Cup – SP / Brazil
- 2006 / May – Champion of National Brazilian Competition / Middleweight – RJ / Brazil
- 2006 / May – Champion of National Brazilian Competition / Open Weight – RJ / Brazil
- 2006 / June – Champion Professional Submission League – LA / California
- 2006 / July – World Champion of Brazilian Jiu-Jitsu / Middleweight / Third Place Open Weight
- 2006 / Nov – Champion II Professional Submission League – LA / California
- 2006 / Nov – Champion Ground Fight Superfight tournament – Houston / Texas
- 2007 / Feb – Champion Grapplers Quest Best of the East – Madison / NJ
- 2007 / Feb – Champion Superfight "Luta Casada" – Rio de Janeiro / Brazil
- 2007 / May – Defending Champion of ADCC – Submission Grappling – up to 76 kilos – Awarded most technical fighter – Trenton / NJ

Employing the butterfly guard against Diego Sanchez, ADCC, 2005

Utilizing the x-guard against Xande Ribeiro, ADCC, 2005

Competition photos by Alicia Anthony

My match with Kurt Pelligrino in ADCC, 2007

Working to set up the x-guard on Mario Miranda, ADCC, 2007

Using the x-guard against Mario Miranda, ADCC, 2007

THE X-GUARD

Back in the early days of my jiu-jitsu career, I spent a lot of time on my back with my opponents in my guard. I got quite good at locking in submissions from this position, especially the triangle choke, but I wasn't very consistent. I would often make mistakes that either cost me points on the judges' scorecards or put me in a vulnerable spot. Not content with this, I decided that I wanted to find a guard that was not only highly effective, but also involved little risk. Instead of a guard that worked some of the time, I wanted a guard that worked most of the time. It had to work on small guys, big guys, short guys, and tall guys. And when I say 'work,' I mean a guard system that would get me from the bottom position to the top position.

The reason I wanted to find a guard that would take me from the bottom to the top was because Brazilian Jiu-Jitsu was not the mystical martial art it had been back when Royce Gracie was first competing in the Ultimate Fighting Championship. It had become as common as karate. There were a number of effective submissions that you could execute from the guard, such as the triangle and armbar, but most competitors had learned how to defend against those submissions. I figured that if I spent all my time developing excellent submissions from the guard, and then went up against an opponent who was a master at defending against those submissions, I could find myself in some trouble. It seemed wiser to focus on escaping the bottom position and rack up some points in the process.

In an attempt to find a guard that suited all my desires, I began playing around with as many types of guards as possible. I liked the regular open guard because it drastically increased my offensive options. The downside was that it also increased my opponent's offensive options. Every time I played the regular open guard, I found myself in compromising situations. Such an outcome happened less frequently when I adopted the spider guard, but due to my inflexibility, I seriously injured my knees on several occasions.

Trying to move forward, I began to work a lot from butterfly guard, and it fit me really well. Every time I made a mistake, I looked at what I had done and attempted to fix it. Sometimes that required me to add elements from other guard styles into my butterfly guard game. Slowly, my butterfly guard began to evolve, and after a couple of years of trial and error, I wound up with the x-guard.

I tested it out against an assortment of competitors in tournaments, and I had a lot of success. A part of that success had to do with the uniqueness of the position. Unlike the triangle and armbar submissions from the guard, few jiu-jitsu practitioners had seen the x-guard, which meant they had little to no defense against it. This was true when competing in Brazilian Jiu-Jitsu competitions, and it was also true when I began entering no-gi tournaments in the United States. The x-guard worked especially well against wrestlers. Most of them are a lot more comfortable working from the top position, and the x-guard allowed me to take them out of their element and put them on their backs. Finishing a wrestler from such a position is much easier than trying to catch him in a triangle from the guard, a submission all wrestlers have learned how to defend against.

Liking the results of the experiment, I immediately focused on developing a reaction for every action my opponent could make while in my x-guard. I did this by testing out each of my possible reactions in a given scenario over and over again during training and while in competition. Whichever reaction posed the least amount of risk and took me to the most advantageous position ended up in my repertoire.

The next step was to alter each of my reactions depending upon my opponent's skill set, weight, flexibility, and a host of other factors. Even when I had found the perfect reaction to pull out on the various types of opponents when they made a specific action in my x-guard, I still occasionally altered my reaction during training just to make sure there wasn't a more effective way to accomplish the same goal. After that, I worked on developing reactions based upon my opponent's counters to my initial reaction. Even if my opponent managed to block three or four sweeps in a row, I wanted to have another sweep waiting for him right around the corner.

As the x-guard evolved, I quickly learned that one of the most wonderful things about the position is you almost always know what your opponent is thinking. You gain such good control of your opponent when you establish the position, it's like you turn him into a puppet on strings. You can feel his every movement, and as long as you understand what techniques are available to you based on his movement, sweeping your opponent becomes the easiest thing in the world.

Despite all my labor, it wasn't until I began using the x-guard to sweep black belts and other competitors who possessed a very high skill level that I realized it wasn't just some random position—it was the guard I had been searching for. This elevated my confidence, and pretty soon it didn't matter whom I was going up against. I knew that if I could get my opponent in the x-guard, I was going to either sweep or submit him.

After having a good deal of success with the x-guard, it's what I became known for. People would constantly ask me questions about how to set up the position, as well as how to execute the various sweeps. When they asked, I could only say one thing, "I know how to do it, but I'm not sure that I can explain it."

I wasn't trying to keep the position all to myself—I honestly didn't know exactly how I did what I did. Each of the reactions I had developed had been on a subconscious level. I knew when I did something right, and I could pull that same reaction out time and again, but if someone were to sit me down and have me take him through the steps, I was lost.

Not wanting to constantly brush people off, I began breaking the position down on a more conscious level, and that's when I truly started to develop the x-guard system that you will find in this book. If it wasn't for people being interested in the x-guard, I honestly don't know if the position would have evolved this far. That's why I'll never consider the x-guard a position I developed. I consider anyone who has ever asked me an x-guard question a contributor. And besides, there might have been a jiu-jitsu practitioner somewhere else in the world developing the exact same guard game at the exact same time.

The x-guard has become my go-to position, but I don't recommend this to everyone. If you already have a guard system that works for you most of the time, you should stick with it. However, just because you have a guard system that works doesn't mean you should ignore the x-guard. It can be an essential tool to have in your arsenal for those times when your opponent manages to shut down your game.

For example, if you're a master at the butterfly guard, you should work for your sweeps from that position first and foremost. But if you run into trouble with your sweeps and you have a good understanding of the x-guard position, it's just an easy transition away. I've seen a lot of jiu-jitsu practitioners begin practicing the x-guard with those intentions—to have the position serve as a fail-safe when their guard game doesn't pan out. As they get deeper and deeper into the x-guard system many realize they have been taking the long route to get the sweep. By going to the x-guard right off the bat, they can get their desired result much quicker.

One of the nicest traits of the x-guard is that you can get it from just about anywhere—all you have to do is develop good timing. Such a goal can take years, but for me it has been well worth the investment. I can recall numerous matches where I was losing pretty significantly, either because I was exhausted or my opponent was constantly on the attack to prevent me from transitioning to the x-guard. If I had just dabbled in the x-guard, I never would have been able to reach the position, but that wasn't the case. At one point in each of these matches my eyes lit up because I knew that for a split second I had an opportunity to assume the x-guard. It suddenly didn't matter to me that I was exhausted or my opponent was bigger and stronger than me—I knew I would come out on top because my timing informed me the x-guard was attainable. I understood that the instant I reached the position, I could take away my opponent's base, and without a base, everyone is the same. It makes the big guy light and the exceptionally quick guy common. How your opponent reacts to the position determines how you're going to get the sweep or submission. If he stands up, you have a reaction. If he leans his weight forward, you have a reaction. If he lets you grab his arm, you have a reaction. No matter how he behaves, you have a reaction. It doesn't matter if you're up against a jiu-jitsu champion or an Olympic wrestler—they all fall for the same techniques.

A perfect example fresh in my mind is my fight with Renzo Gracie in the ADCC World Submission Grappling Championships 2003. I'm pretty certain he had seen me compete because the first two times I attempted to get him in my x-guard, he quickly ran away from the position by backing out. The battle went back and forth for a spell, and then I managed to snare him in the x-guard on my third attempt. Although to Renzo and those watching it might not have looked like I accomplished anything special, I knew it was the most important moment in the fight because I had just established dominance. If I had played butterfly guard or spider guard, two positions Renzo had spent his life developing, the chances are he would have countered every sweep I threw at him. But because the x-guard puts every opponent on the same unfamiliar playing field, I managed to sweep a jiu-jitsu legend and get the win.

The x-guard also gives you options to work around your opponent's strengths. The time I fought Otto Olsen in the ADCC World Submission Grappling Championships 2003 finals is a good example. Prior to the match, I had heard about his phenomenal wrestling ability from numerous sources. I hadn't spent much time on the wrestling mats at that point, and I knew that there was no way that I could come out on top if I played his game. As we drew close, I shot in for a single, but instead of trying to take him down, which would have been a very difficult feat to accomplish, I went straight to the guard.

Instantly I got excited because I had avoided his takedown. It turned out we had gone off the mat and they restarted us in a different position, putting me back to square one, but having spent a lot of time working the x-guard setups you'll find in this book, I managed to quickly pull him back into the position, get the sweep, and obtain the top position. If I hadn't been proficient with the x-guard, I most likely would have had to play Olsen's game, which probably wouldn't have worked out to my advantage.

Another strong example of how the x-guard can come to your aid is my 2006 Mundials fight with Andre Galvao, whom I had defeated three times before. In each of our previous matches he had pulled me into his guard first, and I had passed his guard and gained control of the fight. I went into our fourth match feeling confident because I expected him to do the exact same thing, but that wasn't the case. As we squared off, I kept thinking to myself, "Why isn't he pulling me into his guard?" Instead of finding out what he had on his feet, I immediately pulled him into my x-guard and got the sweep, which landed me back in the same fight I had been in three times before. I never figured out if he was a master at passing the guard because I didn't put myself into a position to find out.

The reason I've been successful with the x-guard is because I've put in the time. Even now, I spend a large portion of my training day working to perfect my game. If you've picked up this book with the intention of learning one or two x-guard moves, it won't get you very far. As you now know, your sweeps and submissions from x-guard are based upon how your opponent reacts to the position. If you don't know all of the options, you will not be effective with the position. In order to get the most out of it, you have to make a firm decision that you are going to learn all the variables and intricacies involved. You have to make a resolute decision to learn the entire x-guard system.

I spent a considerable amount of energy figuring out the best x-guard setups, sweeps, and submissions, and I've laid them all out over the coming pages. If you're serious about becoming proficient with the x-guard, I suggest running over the various techniques in your mind even when you aren't physically training. That's how I developed the system, and it's going to be how you master it. Along the way, you'll probably also see how you can tweak the various techniques to make them more applicable to you. It's not necessary to do the moves exactly how I do them. You might have to change the x-guard to fit your game or you might need to change your game to fit the x-guard. I'm not going to try and convince you which is the better route—that is up to you to decide. However, it's important to realize that jiu-jitsu is different from karate in that it's not important that everyone learn the same kata. The way to progress in jiu-jitsu is to alter a technique you're having trouble with so that it works perfectly for your individual traits and style.

Once you've learned all of your options from the x-guard, it's also important to spend a ton of time in the position to get comfortable with it and develop the strength that it requires. It's not enough to understand how the sweeps are done—you've also got to put in some serious numbers. Today there are many competitors who are extremely athletic, and in order to utilize the x-guard on such opponents, you have to have a lot of strength in your legs and abs. You need to learn how to stay tight and keep your legs strong for a considerable amount of time, and the only way you can acquire these traits is by spending as much time in the x-guard as possible. A good comparison is the triangle from closed guard. If you understand how the submission is done but you never spend any time practicing it, the first time you slap it on an athletic opponent who understands how to resist against it, your legs will get tired in thirty seconds and you'll have to let go of the submission. The same goes for the x-guard. You have to develop the type of strength necessary to get the sweeps that are available to you.

Putting in the numbers will also increase your x-guard confidence, which is the key to success. When I first started playing around with the position, I failed to use it effectively all the time. A large reason for those failures was a lack of confidence. I figured that since I was the only one using the x-guard, it couldn't be that good. Anytime I had a chance to set-up the x-guard, I'd hesitate, sometimes causing the opportunity to pass me by. I could have easily abandoned the position, but determination caused me to stick with it. After time, I started using the sweeps effectively, which in turn caused my confidence to grow. And every time my confidence climbed another rung, I would become more successful with the position. I've now developed a mind-set that the x-guard cannot fail, and it rarely does.

A good way to develop that confidence is to check your ego at the door during training. If you handle every match in the gym as a competition, you'll use the moves that you are already good at, defeat your sparring partners, and go home without having gained much. You have to accept that failure is just a part of growth. If I hadn't made myself vulnerable when developing the x-guard system, I never would have learned how to sweep my opponent based on his weight, skill set, flexibility, and strength. I never would have come up with new moves based upon my training partners counters to the moves I was already doing. To become proficient at the x-guard, you must realize that experimentation and failure is an important part of the learning curve.

BUTTERFLY GUARD

BASIC POSITIONING & GRIP DEFENSE

Before you dive into butterfly guard sweeps or the x-guard system, it is important that you learn basic positioning and defensive tactics. In the section that follows, you'll find rudimentary control positions, multiple options for breaking your opponent's grips, and grip modifications that are imperative when making the transition from gi to no-gi grappling. If you don't take the time to learn these aspects, you will have a lot of trouble sweeping your opponent from the butterfly guard or establishing the x-guard.

BUTTERFLY GUARD STANCE

The butterfly guard stance is an excellent position to assume anytime you're sitting in front of a standing or kneeling opponent because it allows you to stay mobile. With your hands and feet positioned out in front, you can prevent your opponent from establishing grips, back away from his guard passes, or close the distance to assume some form of dominant control, whether it be a collar grip, a sleeve grip, a cross arm grip, or double underhooks. If your stance is weak, both your offense and defense will suffer, making all the various sweeps and submissions I show over the course of the book difficult to manage. For this reason, developing a strong and aggressive butterfly guard stance should be the first task on your agenda.

To assume a proper butterfly guard stance, curl your legs inward until they're bent at a ninety-degree angle, lean forward so that your shoulders and head are in line with your knees, position your elbows to the inside of your knees, and extend your hands out in front of you. This positioning not only allows you to attack, but also defend should your opponent attempt to control your head, collar, wrist, sleeve, or legs.

GI NO-GI   BUTTERFLY GUARD

HAND CONTROL

As a rule of thumb, you never want to let your opponent gain control of your legs, sleeves, wrists, head, or collar because it makes you vulnerable to attack. To prevent this from happening, assume a proper stance and make your hands your first line of defense by keeping them positioned out in front of you. Anytime your opponent reaches for one of your extremities, intercept his attack with your hands and redirect his arm away from the limb he's trying to control. If your opponent manages to sneak his hands past your lines of defense and establish a hold, his offensive options increase dramatically. In such a situation, you want to immediately break his grip, which I demonstrate how to do next.

1. I've assumed the butterfly guard stance. John is down on his knees, looking for an opening to attack.

2. In an attempt to control my right leg, John reaches his left hand toward my right pant sleeve. Before he can establish a grip, I cup my right hand around his left wrist and move his arm away from my leg.

3. John reaches his right hand toward my left collar. To nullify his attack, I cup my left hand around his right wrist and move his arm away from my collar.

BREAKING INSIDE PANT SLEEVE GRIP GI  NO-GI

A lot of jiu-jitsu practitioners will work to achieve an inside leg grip by latching on to the lower portion of your pant sleeve. If your opponent manages to establish this point of control, you want to shatter his hold before he can mount an attack. This can be achieved by cupping the outside of his wrist with your hand, and then simultaneously pulling his arm toward the center of your body and kicking your snared leg away from your body. It is important to note that if you're not wearing a gi and your opponent grips the inside of your ankle with an inverted grip, you can use the same technique to break his hold.

1. John has sneaked his left hand past my defenses and established a grip on the inside of my right pant sleeve.

2. I cup my right hand around the outside of John's left wrist.

3. To break John's grip on my right pant leg, I force his left arm upward using my right hand and extend my right leg away from my body.

BASIC POSITIONING & GRIP DEFENSE   29

BUTTERFLY GUARD  GI NO-GI

BREAKING INSIDE LEG GRIP

In this sequence I demonstrate how to break your opponent's hold when he reaches his arm between your legs and grips the inside of your pant leg just above the knee. The moment he gets his hold, you want to wrap your near arm around his wrist to trap it in the crook of your arm. Once accomplished, shattering his grip is as simple as yanking your arm toward your torso.

1 John has sneaked his left hand past my guard and established a grip on the inside of my right pant leg.

2 In order to get my offense going, I need to break John's grip. To begin, I wrap my right arm around the outside of his left wrist.

3 To break John's grip, I pull my right forearm toward my torso.

BREAKING OUTSIDE LEG GRIP GI  NO-GI

Below I demonstrate how to break an outside leg grip. The defense is quite simple—jam the outside of your near forearm into your opponent's wrist, and then shatter his hold by extending your arm outward. It doesn't matter if your opponent latches on to the outside of your pant leg up by your knee or down by your ankle; the technique is done the same. It can also be used for no-gi grappling when your opponent reaches around your foot and grips your heel.

1 John has established a grip on the outside of my right pant leg.

2 To begin the process of breaking John's grip, I jam my right forearm against the inside of his left wrist.

3 To break John's grip, I drive my right forearm at a downward angle into his left wrist. Notice how I use the sharp edge of my outer forearm to cut through his grip.

BUTTERFLY GUARD

 BUTTERFLY GUARD

BREAKING COLLAR GRIP

There are many ways to break a collar grip, but I find this technique to be the most effective. To begin, isolate the hand your opponent is grabbing your collar with by latching onto his wrist with both of your hands. To break his grip, lean your body backward while applying outward pressure with your arms. Although the technique is quite simple, it is important that you execute it with speed. Drill it as much as possible so that the instant your opponent latches onto your collar, you instinctually isolate his hand and break his grip before he can continue with his attack.

John has sneaked his right hand past my guard and established a grip on my left collar.

To set myself up to break John's grip, I grab the inside of his right wrist with my right hand and then grab the outside of his right wrist with my left hand. Notice how both of my thumbs are wrapped underneath his wrist while my fingers are wrapped over the top. Next, I place my left foot on his right hip.

To break John's grip on my left collar, I lean backward, push his right hand away from my body using both hands, and extend my left foot into his right hip.

BASIC POSITIONING & GRIP DEFENSE 31

COLLAR AND SLEEVE CONTROL

To establish collar and sleeve control from the butterfly guard stance, you simply need to reach your arms forward and latch onto your opponent's jacket. Since it's a linear attack with short distance to cover, your opponent has less time to react than when you drop your hands to form a grip on his pant leg. It can still be quite challenging getting past your opponent's hands, especially if he's an experienced grip fighter, but the reward is well worth the battle. Once you've got your grip, the positioning of your hands gives you the ability to push on your opponent, pull on him, or turn his upper body like a wheel. With such good control over his body, you have numerous options for setting up a sweep or a transition to the x-guard.

To secure collar and sleeve control, I grab Frank's left collar with my right hand and grab the back of his right sleeve just above his elbow with my left hand. It is important to notice the specifics behind each grip. For the collar grip, I coil my thumb around the inside of his lapel and wrap my fingers around the outside. To establish the grip on his arm, I pinch the seam running down the back of his sleeves between my fingers and palm.

COLLAR GRIP VARIATIONS

When you're fighting to gain control of your opponent's collar from the butterfly guard, it doesn't matter which side of his collar you grab. For example, if you're working to grip his lapel with your right hand, you can latch on to either his left or right collar. Some jiu-jitsu practitioners will argue that you can't execute a sweep when you're gripping your opponent's right collar with your right hand, but this is not the case; the sweep is executed exactly the same. The goal is to establish your grip as fast as possible, which can be a daunting task, especially when your opponent has sharp defense. If you manage to grab his right collar with your right hand, don't attempt to better your grip. Instead, keep your grip and put your focus into executing the sweep.

 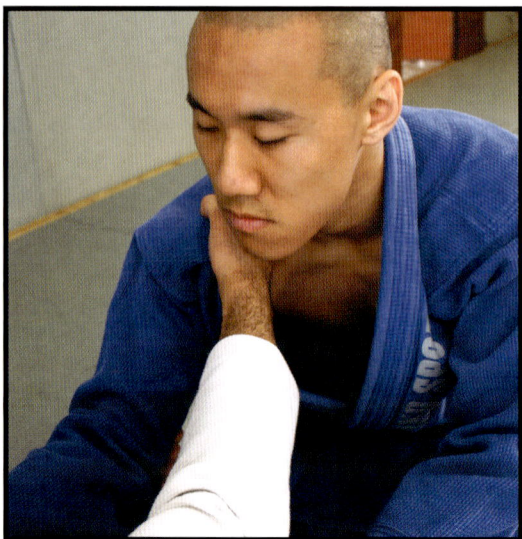

I form a right grip on John's left collar by coiling my thumb around the inside of his lapel and wrapping my fingers around the outside.

I form a right grip on John's right collar by wrapping my fingers around the inside of his lapel and coiling my thumb around the outside.

HEAD AND ARM CONTROL

Head and arm control is the no-gi version of collar and sleeve control. The only difference is that instead of latching on to your opponent's uniform, you cup one hand around the back of his head and grip the back of his triceps with your opposite hand. Establishing this control allows you to sweep your opponent from the butterfly guard or transition to the x-guard, but because your grips aren't as secure as collar and sleeve control, the techniques you can execute are more limited. In order to be effective with the techniques that are at your disposal, you must utilize speed and have no hesitation.

To secure head and arm control, I cup my right hand around the back of Glen's head and grab his right triceps just above his elbow with my left hand.

BASIC POSITIONING & GRIP DEFENSE

BUTTERFLY GUARD 👍 GI 👎 NO-GI

DOUBLE UNDERHOOK CONTROL

Establishing double underhooks gives you complete control of your opponent's upper body, making it a very dominant position. However, obtaining double underhooks often proves quite difficult. The trick is becoming proficient at breaking the distance between you and your opponent and pummeling your arms underneath his arms before he has a chance to react. If you don't put in the necessary practice, the x-guard setups and butterfly sweeps that depend upon double underhook control become obsolete. Below, I demonstrate how to lock your arms in place and secure the position. With the gi version, you want to grab ahold of the fabric covering your opponent's shoulders. In the no-gi version, you cup your hands over his shoulders.

To establish double underhook control with the gi, I slide both of my arms underneath John's arms, anchor my hands in place by clinching the loose fabric on his back in my fists, and then flare my elbows out slightly to prevent him from swimming one of his hands to the inside of my arms and breaking my control by creating distance.

DOUBLE UNDERHOOK CONTROL (NO-GI VARIATION) 👍 GI 👍 NO-GI

To establish double underhook control without the gi, I dive both of my arms underneath Glen's arms, cup my hands over the back of his shoulders, and then flare my elbows out slightly to prevent him from swimming one of his hands to the inside of my arms and breaking my control by creating distance.

CROSS ARM GRIP

The cross arm grip is another excellent form of control that can be used to setup the x-guard or sweep your opponent from the butterfly guard. As you will see throughout the book, I utilize this control often due to its simplicity and effectiveness.

1

John reaches his right hand forward, but before he can establish a grip that could possibly help him pass my guard, I intercept his arm by latching onto his right wrist with my left hand.

2

I double up on John's right arm by pinching the edge of his sleeve between my right index finger and thumb.

3

Having pinched the edge of John's sleeve between my right index finger and thumb, I establish a tight cross grip by wrapping the rest of the fingers on my right hand around the elevated fabric.

BASIC POSITIONING & GRIP DEFENSE

CROSS ARM GRIP TO ARM DRAG

If you watch some of my fights, you'll notice that I utilize arm drags on a regular basis. I use them in numerous butterfly sweeps and x-guard setups, all of which I'll demonstrate how to do over the course of the book. However, before you dig into those techniques, it is important to master the basic arm drag that I've laid out below. If you don't have this technique ingrained into the back of your mind, you'll have a very difficult time pulling off moves based upon the arm drag in later sections.

Babs is posting on his left knee and right foot, looking for an opening to pass my guard. To establish a cross grip, I latch onto his right wrist with my right hand.

As I pull Babs' right arm toward my right side, I extend my legs between his legs, drive my heels into the mat, and then scoot my butt toward my feet to close the distance between us. At the same time, I latch onto the back of his right triceps using my left hand.

Maintaining control of Babs' right arm using my left hand, I release my grip on his wrist, dive my right hand underneath his right arm, and quickly wrap my fingers and thumb of my right hand around the outside of his triceps.

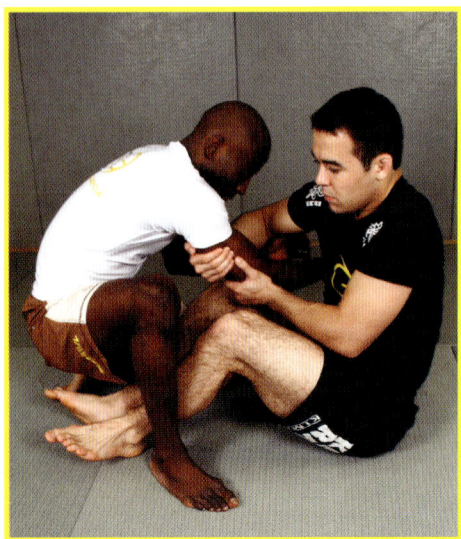

BUTTERFLY GUARD

SWEEPS AND TRANSITIONS

Early in my jiu-jitsu career I began utilizing the butterfly guard on a regular basis, and it played a huge roll in my evolution and my discovery of the x-guard. In this section, I've laid out the sweeps that I've had the most success with. Taking the time to learn each one will not only fill your arsenal with an array of effective techniques that allow you to keep your opponent constantly guessing, but it will also make you more proficient at establishing the x-guard. The majority of the sweeps are based upon an opponent's reaction to your initial attack and sequenced accordingly, so I strongly recommend tackling this section from the beginning.

COLLAR AND SLEEVE CONTROL BUTTERFLY SWEEP

In order to successfully sweep your opponent from the butterfly guard, you first need to establish some type of control over his body. There are many ways to accomplish this, but in this particular technique you're going to use sleeve and collar control, which is perhaps one of the easiest grips to obtain. As I have already mentioned, if you reach for your opponent's collar with your right hand, it doesn't matter if you grab his left lapel or his right lapel; either grip will work just fine. Once you've got a solid grip, the next step is to place one of your feet on your opponent's thigh. If you're gripping his arm with your left hand, then you will place your left foot on his right thigh. If you're gripping his arm with your right hand, you place your right foot on his left thigh. This allows you to kick your opponent's leg out from underneath him, sweep him in the direction of his trapped arm, and establish the top position. It's not always the easiest technique to pull off, but if you move swiftly and have the element of surprise, your opponent will be lying on his back, trying to figure out what just happened. It is important to note that when executing this sweep you can transition into either side control or the mount. Deciding which transition to make should be based upon your opponent's reaction to the sweep and which position you feel most comfortable working from.

1

John is down on his knees, looking for an opening to pass my guard.

2

To pull off a successful sweep, I need to close the distance between John and me and move into his comfort zone. I begin this process by extending both of my legs so that my feet are positioned between his knees. At the same time, I grip his left collar with my right hand and latch onto the back of his right triceps with my left hand.

BUTTERFLY GUARD

3

Pulling John's collar and right arm toward me using my hands, I drive my feet into the mat and scoot my butt toward my heels. The instant I close the distance and move into his comfort zone, I place my left foot on his right thigh just above his knee.

4

Still pulling John's collar and right arm toward me using my hands, I drop to my back and extend my left foot into his right thigh. Notice how my right foot is hooked to the inside of his left thigh.

5

As I drop all the way down to my back, I continue to pull on John's collar and right arm with my hands and extend my left leg into his right thigh. Notice how John's right leg is forced behind him, stripping his base on that side.

SWEEPS & TRANSITIONS 39

BUTTERFLY GUARD

6

In one fluid motion, I roll onto my left hip, draw John's right arm toward me using my left hand, pull up on his left collar with my right hand, and drive my right butterfly hook into his left hip.

7

I continue to roll over onto my left hip, draw John's right arm toward me using my left hand, and pull up on his left collar using my right hand. As John gets swept to his back, I sprawl my left leg straight back and position my right shin across his hips. It is important to notice that I've removed my right butterfly hook, which will allow me to transition to the knee on belly position. If I wanted to transition to the mount position, which I demonstrate in the following technique, I would have kept my right butterfly hook intact.

8

I sweep John over to his back and secure the knee on belly position by pinning his right collar to the mat using my right hand, laying my right shin across his hips, and posting my left knee on the mat.

HEAD AND ARM CONTROL BUTTERFLY SWEEP

This technique is the no-gi version of the previous sweep. Instead of establishing collar and sleeve control, you utilize head and arm control. If you decide to control your opponent's head with your right hand, you want to wrap your right wrist around the back of his neck and position your right forearm in front of his shoulder to effectively control his upper body. With your left hand, you're going to grip his triceps just above his elbow so that your thumb is wrapped around the outside of his arm and your fingers are wrapped around the inside, giving you the ability to trap his arm and prevent him from posting his hand on the mat as you execute the sweep. Another detail worth noting about the photos below is the finish. Instead of ending up in side control as you did in the previous technique, you're going to transition to the mount. In both sweeps, either transition is possible. Deciding which one to utilize should be based upon your opponent's reaction to the sweep and your preference. However, transitioning to the mount usually presents more risk because your opponent can use the momentum of the sweep to roll you to your back. If you don't feel like you have complete control of the situation, moving into side control is generally the safer option.

1 I've closed the distance between Glen and me and secured the butterfly guard with head and arm control. Notice how I'm controlling his right arm by gripping just above his elbow with my left hand, and controlling his head by cupping my right wrist around the back of his neck.

2 I place my left foot on Glen's right thigh just above his knee.

BUTTERFLY GUARD

3. Pulling Glen's head and left arm toward me to control his posture, I drop to my back and drive my left foot into his right thigh. Notice how instead of falling straight back I've fallen slightly to my left side.

4. Continuing to drive my left foot into Glen's right thigh and pull his head and arm toward me, I roll onto my left hip and elevate his leg off the mat using my right butterfly hook.

5. To sweep Glen over to his back, I continue to roll onto my left hip, elevate his left leg off the mat using my right butterfly hook, drive my left foot into his right thigh, and pull his head and right arm toward me.

BUTTERFLY GUARD

6

I continue to drive Glen over to his back.

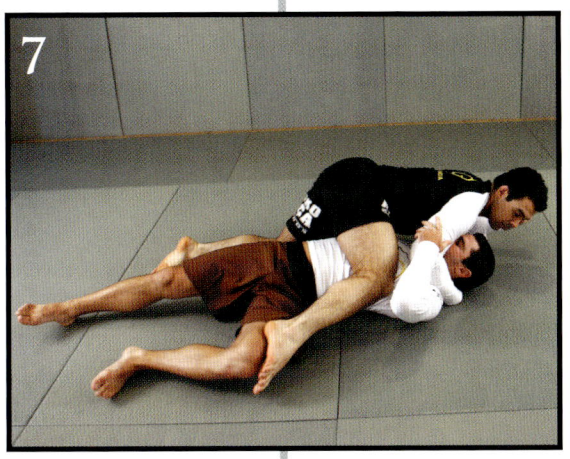

7

As Glen gets forced to his back, I work to secure the mount position by moving my right leg over his torso.

8

To secure the mount position, I drop my right knee to the mat on Glen's left side and plant my right knee on the mat on his right side.

SWEEPS & TRANSITIONS

COLLAR AND SLEEVE CONTROL BUTTERFLY SWEEP 2

This technique is very similar to the collar and sleeve control butterfly sweep. You establish the same grips, sweep your opponent in the same direction, and finish in the knee on belly position. The only difference here is your opponent's leg positioning. Instead of being on both knees, he posts one foot on the mat, which is a common posture among jiu-jitsu practitioners trying pass your guard. To deal with this new scenario, get as close to him as possible, place your foot on his posted leg, and then drive your foot into his leg to stretch him out and destroy his base. Once accomplished, you can sweep your opponent to the mat just as you did in the previous two sequences.

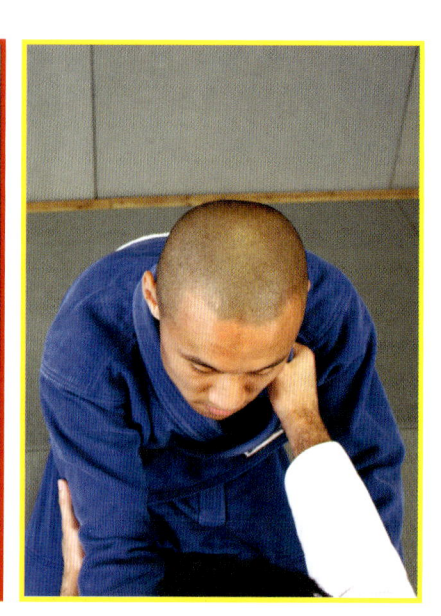

1. I've secured the butterfly guard with collar and sleeve control.

2. John posts his right foot on the mat.

BUTTERFLY GUARD

3 The instant John posts his right foot on the mat, I place my left foot just above his knee on his right thigh.

4 Pulling John toward me using my grips on his collar and right arm, I drop to my back.

5 Still pulling John into me, I drive my left foot into his right thigh and force his leg straight back.

SWEEPS & TRANSITIONS   45

BUTTERFLY GUARD

6

In one fluid motion, I roll onto my left hip, post my left elbow on the mat, pull John's right sleeve toward me using my left hand, pull up on his left collar using my right hand, and elevate his left leg using my right butterfly hook.

7

To sweep John to his back, I continue to roll over onto my left hip, pull his right sleeve into me using my left hand, pull up on his left collar with my right hand, and elevate his left leg using my right butterfly hook.

8

To secure the knee on belly position, I lay my right shin across his hips, pin his right collar to the mat using my right hand, and post my left knee on the mat.

46 BUTTERFLY GUARD

ANKLE PICK BUTTERFLY SWEEP

The ankle pick butterfly sweep is a simple, low-risk technique that works great against an opponent who is posted on one knee and one foot. The goal is to pull his posted leg out from underneath him and then push his weight toward that side. When done correctly, it's like removing a leg from a table and then placing a heavy object on that corner. One second your opponent is looking for an opening to pass your guard, and the next he's lying on his back.

1

I'm sitting on my butt with both of my hands positioned out in front of me. Glen is posting on his right knee and left foot, looking for an opening to pass my guard.

2

I grab Glen's left wrist with my right hand.

SWEEPS & TRANSITIONS

BUTTERFLY GUARD

3

In order to sweep Glen to the mat, I first need to close the distance and move into his comfort zone. To begin the process, I extend both of my legs so that my feet are positioned between his legs.

4

To close the distance, I pull on Glen's left wrist with my right hand, drive my feet into the mat, and scoot my butt toward my heels. As I move into Glen's comfort zone, I place my left hand on the right side of his neck.

5

I push on Glen's neck with my left hand, release my right grip on his wrist, and grab his left ankle with my right hand.

BUTTERFLY GUARD

BUTTERFLY GUARD

6

Still pushing on Glen's neck with my left hand, I pull his left ankle toward me using my right hand and come up onto my right knee.

7

Still driving my left hand into Glen's neck, I pull his left ankle to my right hip using my right hand.

8

As Glen gets swept to his back, I pin my left knee to his left hip, place my right hand on his left thigh, and prepare to pass his guard.

SWEEPS & TRANSITIONS 49

BUTTERFLY GUARD 👍 GI 👎 NO-GI

DOUBLE UNDERHOOK BUTTERFLY SWEEP

A lot of times when you work to establish double underhooks from the butterfly guard, you'll end up with one underhook, and your opponent will end up with one underhook. This is a neutral position. Although you can still execute a sweep, you don't have optimal control over your opponent's body. To avoid this even playing field, invest the time it takes to become a master at establishing double underhooks. Once accomplished, securing this dominant hold in a fight will allow you to effortlessly lift your opponent's body into the air, giving you a plethora of options. You can utilize the sweep below, one of the other sweeps laid out in this section, or make an easy transition to the x-guard, which I'll demonstrate later. Without double underhooks, you're going to have a much harder time imposing your will from the butterfly guard.

1

John is down on his knees, looking for an opening to pass my guard.

2

To begin closing the distance between John and me, I extend both of my legs so that my feet are positioned between his legs. Next, I drive my feet into the mat and scoot my butt toward my heels. As I move into his comfort zone, I reach both of my arms underneath his armpits. It is important to note that this step must be executed with speed to prevent your opponent from countering your movement.

BUTTERFLY GUARD

3

To secure double underhook control, I wrap both of my arms underneath John's arms, secure my hands in place by making a fist around the loose material on the back of his gi, and then flare my elbows out slightly to my sides.

4

Keeping John's torso close to mine by utilizing my double underhook control, I roll back and elevate his hips off the mat using my butterfly hooks.

5

In an attempt to nullify my sweep, John drops both of his feet to the mat. The instant he does this, I remove my left butterfly hook from his right leg and then place my left foot on his right thigh just above his knee.

SWEEPS & TRANSITIONS

BUTTERFLY GUARD

6

To begin sweeping John, I turn onto my left side, drive my left foot into his right thigh, and extend my right butterfly hook into his left leg. Notice that I've maintained control of his upper body by keeping both of my underhooks locked tight. If you lose control of your opponent's upper body, he can potentially block your sweep by posting his arms on the mat.

7

Still controlling John with my double underhooks, I remove my right butterfly hook, roll onto my left hip, and begin working for the knee on belly position.

8

As John is forced to his back, I secure the knee on belly position by sliding my right shin across his hips and positioning my left knee on the mat.

BUTTERFLY GUARD

DOUBLE UNDERHOOK BUTTERFLY SWEEP (NO-GI)

This technique is the no-gi version of the double underhook butterfly sweep. The only significant modification is how you form your grip. Instead of latching on to the loose material above your opponent's shoulders, you cup your hands over the top of his shoulders to secure them in place. Once accomplished, lift your opponent's hips off the mat using your butterfly hooks just as you did previously. If your opponent reacts by dropping his feet to the mat, you can either utilize the sweep shown below or the x-guard transition shown later in the book.

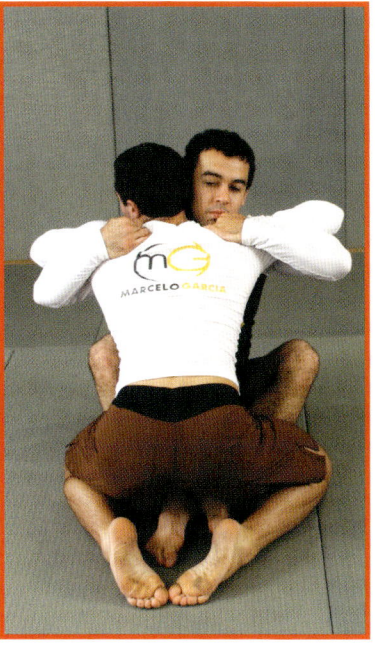

1 I've established the butterfly guard and secured double underhooks. Notice how my elbows are flared out to my sides and I'm cupping my hands around Glen's shoulders. This prevents him from swimming one of his hands to the inside of my arms and breaking my control by creating distance between us.

2 Keeping Glen's torso glued to mine, I roll to my back and use my butterfly hooks to elevate his hips off the mat.

SWEEPS & TRANSITIONS 53

BUTTERFLY GUARD

3

In an attempt to block my sweep and regain his base, Glen drops both of his feet to the mat.

4

The instant Glen drops both of his feet to the mat, I place my left foot on his right thigh.

5

To sweep Glen to the mat, I roll onto my left side, push my left foot into his right leg, and drive my right butterfly hook into his left leg.

54   BUTTERFLY GUARD

BUTTERFLY GUARD

6

I continue to roll onto my left side, push my left foot into Glen's right leg, and drive my right butterfly hook into his left leg.

7

As Glen gets swept to his back, I slide my right knee over his torso.

8

To secure the mount position, I post my right knee on the mat on the left side of Glen's body and post my left knee on the right side of his body.

SWEEPS & TRANSITIONS 55

BUTTERFLY GUARD 👍 GI 👍 NO-GI

DOUBLE UNDERHOOK PUSH BACK SWEEP

As I've mentioned, deciding which sweep to employ should be based upon how your opponent reacts to your initial attack. In the scenario below, you secure double underhooks and lift your opponent off the mat, but instead of dropping his feet to stabilize his position as he did in the previous scenarios, he floats his hips over your butterfly hooks and maintains his balance in the air, preventing you from executing the butterfly sweep. If your opponent chooses to do this, you can rock your body into the sit up position and use the momentum you generate to climb to your feet. To topple your opponent to the mat on your way up, turn your double underhooks into a bear hug by grabbing one of your wrists with your opposite hand and then drive your shoulder into his head. Once you've got him down, it is important to maintain solid pressure with your body lock until you can secure the mount position. If you don't, your opponent will have a chance to recover and put you in his guard.

1

I've established the butterfly guard and secured double underhooks.

2

Keeping John's upper body locked to my chest using my double underhook control, I roll to my back and elevate his hips off the mat using my butterfly hooks.

56 BUTTERFLY GUARD

BUTTERFLY GUARD

3

To prevent me from sweeping him to his back, John floats his weight over the top of my butterfly hooks and works to maintain his balance in the air. His actions give me a couple of options. I can keep him elevated and try to work my various sweep attacks or I can generate momentum by lowering him to the mat and sitting up, which will allow me to climb to my feet. In this sequence, I choose the latter because John is countering my sweeps by keeping his hips low, which will make it fairly easy for me to climb to my feet. As I rock my weight forward, I clasp my hands together in the small of his back.

4

As I rock into the sit-up position, I curl both of my legs inward, plant my feet on the mat underneath my hips, and use my forward momentum to begin standing up.

5

Pressing forward, I climb to my feet. To break John's posture, I pull my clasped hands into the center of his back and push my right shoulder into his head. Notice how this push-pull effect folds him backward.

SWEEPS & TRANSITIONS

BUTTERFLY GUARD

6

Still pressing forward, I step my right foot to the outside of John's left leg.

7

As John collapses to the mat, I walk my legs around the outside of his legs and land in the mount position.

8

I release my double underhook grip, place both hands on the mat, and prepare to attack from the mount position.

HALF BUTTERFLY SWEEP (OFF PUMMEL)

In previous sequences I demonstrated how to close the distance between you and your opponent, secure double underhook control by diving your arms underneath his arms, establish the butterfly guard, and then use your positioning and control to sweep him to his back and secure the top position. It's great when things play out in this manner, but a lot of times as you work to close the distance, your opponent will pummel one of his arms underneath one of your arms, stealing one of your underhooks. In such a situation, the first thing you must do is hold on really tight with your one existing underhook to prevent him from stealing that from you as well. It is also important to understand how to reacquire your double underhooks through pummeling, but it is not mandatory. As long as you can hold on to one underhook, you have a lot of options, such as the sweep I demonstrate here. If your opponent established an underhook with his right arm, you want to pull his right arm in tight to your body with your left hand and then use your right underhook and right butterfly hook to sweep him over to his back. Your opponent will have more ability to recover to guard when executing this sweep, so instead of transitioning into the mount, you should play things safe and transition into side control. Sometimes if you look for too much, you can lose everything.

1

John is down on his knees, looking for an opening to pass my guard.

2

I close the distance by extending my legs, driving my feet into the mat, and scooting my butt toward my heels. As I move into John's comfort zone, I reach both of my arms underneath his armpits to establish double underhooks. However, John counters by swimming his right hand to the inside of my left arm.

BUTTERFLY GUARD

3

As John works to establish an underhook with his right arm, I place my head on his right shoulder, grip his right triceps with my left hand, and then trap his arm by pulling my left elbow tight to my body. At the same time, I wrap my right arm around his back and prepare to fall onto my left hip.

4

As I begin to fall to my left side, I pull down on John's right arm using my left arm and push up on his left arm using my right arm.

5

To elevate John's hips off the mat, I fall to my left side, drive my right butterfly hook up into his left leg, and push off the mat with my left foot. At the same time, I continue to pull down on his right arm using my left arm and drive the left side of his body upward using my right underhook.

BUTTERFLY GUARD

BUTTERFLY GUARD

6

I continue to push off the mat using my left leg and drive my right butterfly hook up into John's left leg.

7

Still pushing off the mat with my left leg and driving my right butterfly hook up into John's left leg, I roll over onto my left shoulder.

8

As John gets flipped over onto his back, I release my right butterfly hook and prepare to transition to side control. Notice how I continue to control his right arm, as well as maintain my right underhook on his left side.

SWEEPS & TRANSITIONS

BUTTERFLY GUARD

9

In order to secure side control, I need to pin John's back to the mat and pass my right leg through his guard. To begin, I post my left foot on the mat, plant my right knee on the mat next to his right hip, and place my right instep over his right thigh.

10

Pulling John's right arm off the mat using my left hand, I slide my right leg underneath my left leg and then position my right knee underneath his left shoulder.

11

To secure side control, I curl my left leg behind me and drop my left knee and hip to the mat.

BUTTERFLY GUARD

STOMP KICK HALF BUTTERFLY SWEEP (OFF PUMMEL)

This technique comes into play when you execute the half butterfly sweep and your opponent counters by posting his foot on the mat. To counter his counter, place your foot on his knee and push his leg out from underneath him. Once accomplished, roll him to his back and assume the top position.

1

John is down on his knees, looking for an opening to pass my guard.

2

Before John can initiate an attack, I straighten my legs, drive my feet into the mat, and scoot my butt toward my heels. As I move into his comfort zone, I attempt to reach my arms underneath his armpits to secure double underhook control.

SWEEPS & TRANSITIONS

BUTTERFLY GUARD

3

As I draw closer to John and work to establish double underhook control, he counters my attack by swimming his right hand to the inside of my left arm.

4

As John pummels his right arm to the inside of my left arm, I place my head on his right shoulder, grip his right triceps with my left hand, and then trap his right arm to my body by sucking my left elbow in tight. At the same time, I reach my right arm around his back and prepare to fall to my left side.

5

As I fall to my left side, I pull down on John's right arm using my left hand, drive my right underhook up into his left armpit, and extend my right butterfly hook into his left leg.

BUTTERFLY GUARD

BUTTERFLY GUARD

6 John counters my 'half butterfly sweep' by posting his right foot on the mat.

7 The instant John posts his right foot on the mat, I place my left foot on the inside of his right thigh.

8 I drive my left foot into John's right leg.

SWEEPS & TRANSITIONS 65

BUTTERFLY GUARD

9

To sweep John to his back, I roll over onto my left hip while continuing to drive my left foot into his right leg, pull down on his right arm using my left arm, and drive my right underhook up into his left armpit.

10

As John gets swept to his back, I roll over on top of him to pin his back to the mat, sprawl my left leg straight back, and place my right instep against the outside of his right hip.

11

To secure the knee on belly position, I keep my right shin pinned to John's hips and slide my left knee up to his right arm.

66 BUTTERFLY GUARD

👍 GI 👎 NO-GI — BUTTERFLY GUARD

CROSS ARM GRIP TO BACK TRANSITION

In this technique I demonstrate how to use a cross arm grip to take your opponent's back from the butterfly guard. To begin the transition, establish a tight hold on your opponent's sleeve, dig your feet into the mat, and pull his arm across your body as you jump your weight backward. The idea is to use your backward momentum to yank your opponent forward. This allows you to pin his captured hand to the mat using your grip on his sleeve, swing around to his back, and secure the back position by establishing over-under control and both of your hooks. If making a transition to his back isn't possible for whatever reason, you can also use a cross arm grip to sweep your opponent from the butterfly guard or set up the x-guard, both of which I'll demonstrate shortly.

1

John is down on his knees, looking for an opening to pass my guard.

2

John reaches his right hand toward my left pant sleeve, but before he can secure his grip, I grab his right wrist with my left hand. Next, I double up on his wrist by pinching the edge of his right sleeve between my right index finger and thumb.

SWEEPS & TRANSITIONS 67

BUTTERFLY GUARD

3

Having pinched the edge of John's sleeve between my right index finger and thumb, I wrap the rest of the fingers on my right hand around the elevated fabric, forming a tight grip.

4

In one fluid motion, I rip John's arm to the right side of my body and drive his hand to the mat. At the same time, I extend my right leg between his legs. This is a very important step because it will allow me to secure my first hook as I swing around behind him and take his back.

5

Still pinning John's right hand to the mat using my right grip on his sleeve, I push off the mat with my left leg and right arm, elevate my hips, and reach my left arm around his back.

BUTTERFLY GUARD

BUTTERFLY GUARD

6

Placing my chest on John's back, I wrap my left arm underneath his left arm. Notice how my right leg is now hooked around the inside of his right leg.

7

To establish over-under control on John's upper body, I release my grip on his sleeve, wrap my right arm around the right side of his neck, and then grab my right wrist with my left hand.

8

To secure control of John's back, I fall onto my right side and wrap my left leg over his left leg.

SWEEPS & TRANSITIONS 69

ARM DRAG REVERSE SWEEP

When you secure a cross grip on your opponent's sleeve and pull his arm across your body, he will often post on one foot to prevent you from taking his back. In such a scenario, a good option is to execute an arm drag to close the distance, wrap your opposite arm around his posted leg, roll backward, and execute a sweep. Speed is a very important aspect with this technique. The instant your opponent posts his foot, you want to transition from taking his back to the sweep. The idea is to move on to an alternate attack while your opponent is still focused on blocking your previous one.

1 John is down on his knees, looking for an opening to pass my guard.

2 I grab John's right wrist with my left hand.

70 BUTTERFLY GUARD

BUTTERFLY GUARD

3

Still controlling John's right wrist with my left hand, I pinch the edge of his right sleeve between my right index finger and thumb.

4

Having pinched the edge of John's right sleeve between my right index finger and thumb, I wrap the other fingers of my right hand around the elevated fabric. Once I have a solid hold, I rotate my right elbow inward to twist his sleeve tighter around his arm and snare his wrist.

5

I place my left hand on John's right triceps and then use both of my hands to pull his right arm across my torso toward the right side of my body. Fearing I might attempt to take his back, John reacts to my attack by posting his right foot on the mat.

SWEEPS & TRANSITIONS

BUTTERFLY GUARD

6

Still controlling John's right arm with my left hand, I release my right grip on his sleeve and wrap my right hand around the inside of his upper right triceps. As soon as I establish this grip, I continue to move his right arm toward the right side of my body by pushing on his triceps with my left hand and pulling on it with my right. At the same time, I straighten my left leg so that it is positioned to the inside of his right foot.

7

Continuing to pull John's right arm toward the right side of my body using my right hand, I release my left grip on his triceps and hook my left arm over the top of his right leg.

8

Still controlling John's right arm and right leg, I fall to my back, push off the mat with my left foot, and extend my right butterfly hook into his left leg.

BUTTERFLY GUARD

BUTTERFLY GUARD

9 — I continue to push off the mat with my left foot and drive my right butterfly hook up into John's left leg, forcing him to roll forward over his right shoulder. Notice how I have maintained tight control of his right arm to prevent him from blocking my sweep by posting his right hand on the mat.

10 — Pushing off my left foot and using the momentum I generated with the sweep, I roll backward over my right shoulder to establish the top position.

11 — Still controlling John's right arm and right leg, I continue to roll backward over my right shoulder and work to establish the top position. Notice how I keep my right hook attached to the inside of his left leg. This prevents him from pulling me into his closed guard as I come down on top of him.

SWEEPS & TRANSITIONS

BUTTERFLY GUARD

12 Rolling over John's body, I drive my left foot toward the mat.

13 To secure the top position, I wrap my left arm around the right side of John's head, post my left hand on the mat, and place my left knee underneath his right buttocks. From here I will work to pass his guard.

GI　NO-GI　BUTTERFLY GUARD

CROSS ARM CONTROL

Earlier in the section I demonstrated several ways to sweep your opponent from the butterfly guard when you establish double underhook control. Although these are high-percentage sweeps, your opponent might realize your intentions as you attempt to close the distance and prevent you from establishing double underhooks by pushing you away with his hands. Being held at bay makes it very difficult to acquire double underhooks, but it allows you to isolate one of your opponent's arms by grabbing his sleeve with one hand and his triceps with your other. Once you've isolated his arm in this manner, you can pull his arm across your body. If you've latched on to your opponent's right arm as I do in the photos below, you'll want to pull his right arm to your right side. If you've grabbed his left arm, you'll pull his left arm to your left side. This disrupts your opponent's base and eliminates his lines of defense, making it easy to close the distance. Once accomplished, your opponent's isolated arm will be trapped between your body and his body. To secure the position, reach the hand you were gripping his triceps with over his back and latch on to his belt. As you will see shortly, assuming this position gives you numerous options to attack.

1 John is down on his knees, looking for an opening to pass my guard.

2 I close the distance by extending my legs, driving my feet into the mat, and scooting my butt toward my heels. As I move into John's comfort zone, he drives his hands into my shoulders to stop my forward progression.

3 The instant John drives his hands into my shoulders, I place my left hand on his right triceps and grab his right wrist using my right hand.

SWEEPS & TRANSITIONS

BUTTERFLY GUARD

4 — To secure control of John's right arm, I lock onto his right triceps using my left hand and make a fist around the loose fabric of his right sleeve using the fingers of my right hand. Once I have a solid grip on his sleeve, I curl my right arm in tight to my body.

5 — Using both hands, I move John's arm across my torso toward the right side of my body.

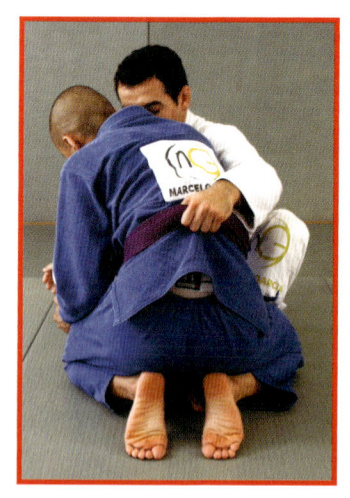

6 — Now that I've moved John's right arm to my right side, I release my left grip on his wrist and pull his arm toward my right hip using my right grip on his sleeve. At the same time, I scoot my butt toward my heels, reach my left arm around his back, and grip his belt with my left hand. Having established cross arm control, I'm in an excellent position to attack.

CROSS ARM CONTROL UNDERHOOK SWEEP

This is a very simple yet effective sweep that you can utilize when you achieve the cross arm control position from butterfly guard. If you have your opponent's right arm trapped as I do in the photos below, you execute the sweep by establishing an underhook on his left side, lifting his body into the air using your butterfly hooks, and then simply rolling to the side of his trapped arm. The trick is keeping your torso glued to your opponent's torso to prevent him from freeing his trapped arm and blocking your sweep by posting his hand on the mat.

1 I've established cross arm control on John.

2 I release my grip on John's sleeve, reach my right arm underneath his left arm, and secure a right underhook by grabbing the loose fabric on the back of his gi with my right hand.

3 Rolling to my back, I lift John's legs off the mat by driving my butterfly hooks upward into his hips.

SWEEPS & TRANSITIONS

BUTTERFLY GUARD

4

As soon as I heft John's legs off the mat, I roll toward my left side. Because I closed the distance between us while his right arm was on the right side of my body, his right arm is now trapped between our torsos, making it impossible for him to block my sweep by posting his right hand on the mat.

5

Keeping my torso locked to John's torso, I continue to roll over to my left side toward the mount position.

6

To secure the mount, I plant my right knee on John's left side and slide both feet underneath the outside of his legs.

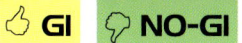

CROSS ARM CONTROL HALF BUTTERFLY SWEEP 1

This is another great sweep that you can utilize from the cross arm control position. If you're controlling your opponent's right sleeve with your right hand as I am in the photos below, release your right butterfly hook, straighten your right leg between your opponent's legs, and dive your body underneath his body. Once you acquire the appropriate angle, force his trapped arm up into his right hip using your right hand, lift his legs off the mat using your left butterfly hook, and pull on his belt with your left hand. When done right and with the proper speed, these actions will cast your opponent over his trapped arm and onto his back.

1 I've established cross arm control on John.

2 I fall to my right side, straighten my right leg out between John's legs, and push his right arm into his left hip using my right grip on his sleeve.

SWEEPS & TRANSITIONS

BUTTERFLY GUARD

3

Keeping my left butterfly hook intact, I roll toward my left shoulder, pull on John's belt with my left hand, and push up on his left hip using my right hand. Because I'm still gripping his right sleeve with my right hand, I accomplish this last action by driving his arm into his own hip.

4

Continuing to pull on John's belt with my left hand and push on his left hip with my right hand, I drive off my right foot and extend my left butterfly hook into his right leg, forcing him to roll forward over his right shoulder.

5

I cast John over his right shoulder by continuing to drive my left butterfly hook into his right leg.

80 BUTTERFLY GUARD

BUTTERFLY GUARD

6

As John lands on his back, I begin sitting up.

7

As I sit up, I begin turning into John.

8

I slide my left leg underneath my right leg, plant my right knee against John's right hip, place my left knee against his right shoulder, and position my chest over his chest. To secure the side control position, I release my right grip on his sleeve, plant my right elbow on the left side of his body, and grip the inside of his left biceps with my right hand.

SWEEPS & TRANSITIONS

CROSS ARM CONTROL HALF BUTTERFLY SWEEP 2

The majority of sweeps I've shown so far can be sequenced together into one continuous attack. If your first sweep doesn't work, move on to the next sweep in the sequence. If your second sweep doesn't work, move onto the third. Understanding where to go based on your opponent's reaction to your attack is an integral part of jiu-jitsu, as is learning which sweeps work on heavier opponents, more flexible opponents, and opponents who have exceptional balance. As long as you understand how to capitalize on your opponent's strengths, weaknesses, and counters, you'll always be able to catch him off guard. With that said, this particular technique comes in handy when you are unable to sweep your opponent with the previous technique because his base is too strong. Instead of giving up on your attack, you establish an underhook on his far leg, which gives you more leverage to finish the sweep.

1 I've established cross arm control on John.

2 I fall to my right side, straighten my right leg out between John's legs, release my right grip on his sleeve, and then hook my right arm underneath his left leg.

BUTTERFLY GUARD

3 In one fluid motion, I roll to my back, pull on John's belt with my left hand, push on his left leg with my right arm, and drive my left butterfly hook up into his right leg.

4 Rolling toward my left side, I continue to pull on John's belt with my left hand, push on his left leg with my right underhook, and drive my left butterfly hook up into his right leg.

5 Continuing with my previous actions, John is forced to roll over his right shoulder.

SWEEPS & TRANSITIONS 83

BUTTERFLY GUARD

6

As John gets swept to his back, I use my left grip on his belt and my right underhook on his left leg to pull myself into the top position.

7

In order to secure the side control position, I need to pin John's shoulders to the mat and position my knees on the right side of his body. To begin, I slide my left leg underneath my right leg. Next, I sprawl my left leg straight back and bring my right knee up to his right hip. Notice how I've maintained my right underhook and my left grip on his belt. This allows me to keep his shoulders pinned to the mat as I get my legs into proper position.

8

I secure side control on John's right side by bringing my left knee up to his right shoulder and setting my weight down on the top of his torso.

CROSS ARM CONTROL REVERSE SWEEP 1

This is the third sweep that you can execute in the current sequence, and it comes into play when your opponent prevents you from utilizing the previous two techniques by stretching his leg and free arm out to his side. In such a situation it is difficult to sweep him toward his trapped arm because all of his weight is distributed on his opposite side. Instead of trying to muscle your opponent over, quickly trap his free arm, lift his body off the mat using your butterfly hook, and sweep him in the opposite direction. If you glance at the photos below, you'll notice that my opponent posts his free arm out to his side up by my head, which allows me to underhook his arm and trap it by pulling it toward my head. If he had posted his arm out to his side down by his waist, I would have pushed down on his arm and trapped it by his hip. To learn how this is done, visit the next technique in this section.

I've established cross arm control on John.

I fall to my right side, straighten my right leg out between John's legs, and drive his right arm into his left hip using my right hand.

SWEEPS & TRANSITIONS

BUTTERFLY GUARD

3

John realizes that I'm trying to sweep him in the direction of his trapped arm. To prevent me from accomplishing my goal, he sprawls his left leg back, posts his left hand, and drops his left hip to the mat. His actions place all of his weight on my right side, making it very difficult for me to sweep him to my left.

4

Although John's counter has hindered me from sweeping him to my left side, I now have an opportunity to sweep him to my right side. To do this, I first need to trap his left arm. Because he has his left arm positioned up by my head, I dig my right arm underneath his left arm and hook my wrist around the back of his elbow. This will allow me to trap his arm by pulling it toward my head. If his left arm were posted lower, I would have hooked my right arm around the outside of his arm and pushed it toward my legs, which I demonstrate how to do in the next sequence.

5

I pull John's left arm to the right side of my neck using my right arm.

THE X-GUARD

BUTTERFLY GUARD

6

The instant I trap John's left arm, I drive my left butterfly hook up into his right leg and follow him over.

7

As I sweep John over to his back using my left butterfly hook, I keep my chest pinned to his right arm. This prevents him from hooking his right arm around my left arm, bridging to his right, and using the momentum of my sweep to roll me to my back.

8

To secure the mount, I move my left foot to the outside of John's right leg.

ESTABLISHING THE X-GUARD

CROSS ARM CONTROL REVERSE SWEEP 2

This is the exact same technique as the previous one; the only difference here is that your opponent posts his hand down by your hips rather than up by your head. Instead of trying to underhook his arm and trap it against your upper body, you push down on his arm and trap it by his hip.

1

I've secured cross arm control on John.

2

I fall to my right side, straighten my right leg out between John's legs, and drive his right arm into his left hip using my right hand. Realizing that I'm going to try to sweep him to my left side, John sprawls his left leg back and posts his left hand on the mat.

88 BUTTERFLY GUARD

BUTTERFLY GUARD

3

Although John's counter has hindered me from sweeping him to my left side, I now have an opportunity to sweep him to my right side. To do this, I first need to trap his left arm. In the previous sequence he posted his left hand up by my head, which allowed me to dig my right arm underneath his left arm, but here he has posted his left hand further down toward my waist. In this scenario, I place my right hand on the outside of his left arm.

4

I push John's left arm toward my legs using my right hand.

5

Pinning John's left arm to his side using my right hand, I drive my left butterfly hook up into his right leg and roll over onto my right side.

SWEEPS & TRANSITIONS

BUTTERFLY GUARD

6

As I force John toward his back by driving my left butterfly hook up into his right leg, I come up onto my right knee.

7

I continue to roll John over to his back by driving his right leg toward the mat using my left butterfly hook. It is important to notice that I've maintained tight control of his upper body, leaving no space for him to scramble.

8

To secure the mount, I place my left knee on the mat on John's right side.

BUTTERFLY GUARD SUBMISSIONS

The butterfly guard doesn't offer a plethora of submissions, but there are a few highly effective ones that can be applied when your opponent presents you with the necessary opening, which usually happens when he attempts to pass your guard. I suggest learning as many submissions from the butterfly guard as possible because the instant you acquire the ability to counter your opponent's attack with an attack of your own, you become a whole lot more dangerous. Without that ability, your guard game is not complete.

BUTTERFLY GUARD 👍 GI 👍 NO-GI

STRAIGHT ARMBAR

The butterfly guard is not the optimal position from which to lock in a submission, but there are a few available when you know what to look for. In this sequence, I demonstrate how to lock in a straight armbar. This technique can either be set up or serve as a counter when your opponent tries to pummel his arm underneath your arm in an attempt to secure an underhook. The key to success in either scenario is timing and speed. Before your opponent can secure an underhook, you must trap his wrist under your armpit by drawing your arm in tight to your body. If you're slow to clamp down and allow him to get his arm deep, the technique won't work. Once you snare his wrist, you can secure the straight armbar by placing your feet on his hips, falling to your back, and thrusting your hips up into his elbow. It's not a very high percentage submission, but it works great when your timing is sharp.

1 John is down on his knees, looking for an opportunity to pass my guard.

2 Before John can initiate an attack, I lift my legs off the mat and place my feet on his hips.

3 Reaching my arms forward, I latch onto John's right triceps with my left hand and work to establish a grip on his left triceps with my right hand. It is important to notice where and how I grip his right arm. My hand is positioned just above his elbow, my fingers are wrapped around the back of his triceps, and my thumb is gripped around the outside of his triceps.

BUTTERFLY GUARD

BUTTERFLY GUARD

4 Keeping my left grip tight, I pull John's right arm toward my body using my left hand. My goal is to move his right wrist underneath my left armpit so I can straighten out his arm and secure the armbar.

5 To prevent John from freeing his right arm, I pinch his arm between my left biceps and ribcage by pulling my elbow tight against my body.

6 Maintaining tight control of John's right arm by keeping my left elbow pinned against my side, I roll to my back and slide my right knee to the front of his left shoulder.

7 To secure the straight armbar, I push off John's right hip using my left foot, pinch my knees together, and elevate my hips into his right elbow.

SUBMISSIONS 93

BUTTERFLY GUARD 👍 GI 👍 NO-GI

TRIANGLE ARMBAR FINISH

It's always good to be the one attacking, but it's also important to understand how to counter your opponent's attack with one of your own. In this scenario, your opponent attempts to pass your guard by pinning one of your legs to the mat. Although this makes it difficult for you to utilize one of your sweeps, it sets you up perfectly to apply the triangle armbar. This can be achieved by latching on to the arm your opponent is using to pin your leg to the mat and swinging your free leg over his shoulder. With just two small movements, you just trapped your opponent's head and one of his arms between your legs. From this position, I will usually transition to the armbar instead of going for the triangle for two reasons. The first is that my legs are short and the armbar is much easier for me to finish, and the other is because most opponents will remain postured up, making it difficult to lock in the triangle.

1

John is on his knees, looking for an opportunity to pass my guard.

2

In an attempt to pass my guard, John charges forward, pushing my left leg to the mat using his right hand and wrapping his left arm around my right leg. I react to his movement by rolling to my back, placing my left foot on his right hip, and grabbing his right triceps with my left hand.

94   BUTTERFLY GUARD

BUTTERFLY GUARD

3

In order to counter John's attack with the triangle armbar submission, I need to first trap his right arm and head between my legs. To begin, I drive my left foot into his right hip, pull his right arm to the front of my left leg using my left hand, move my right foot to the front of his left shoulder, and then push his upper body away from me using my right leg.

4

I pull John's right arm into my left armpit using my left hand, wrap my right leg around the left side of his head, elevate my hips off the mat by pushing off his right hip with my left foot, and clamp my left knee to his right shoulder.

5

I hook my left foot over my right foot and trap John's right wrist underneath my left armpit by pressing my left elbow tight to my body. Notice how this traps his right wrist between my biceps and ribcage. To secure the triangle armbar, I pinch my knees together and elevate my hips into his right elbow.

SUBMISSIONS 95

TRIANGLE FINISH

In the previous sequence I demonstrated how to lock in the triangle armbar when your opponent attempts to pass your guard by pinning one of your legs to the mat. Although it's a great submission, sometimes your opponent will defend by wrapping his trapped arm around your leg. This makes it difficult to lock in the armbar, but it allows you to immediately transition into the triangle. It is important to pay special attention to the photos and captions below because I finish the submission differently than most.

1

I've trapped John's right arm and head between my legs.

2

In order to finish the triangle, I need to position my left leg across the back of John's neck. To begin, I roll to my left side and cup both of my hands around the back of his right arm.

96 BUTTERFLY GUARD

BUTTERFLY GUARD

3 I unhook my feet and slide my left leg up John's back.

4 I wrap my right leg over my left foot, grab my left foot with my right hand, and then pull my left instep into the crook of my right knee.

5 I roll onto my left shoulder and grab the top of my left knee with my right hand. To finish the triangle, I squeeze my knees together and pull my left knee into John's right shoulder using my right hand.

SUBMISSIONS 97

OMOPLATA

When both you and your opponent are tied up in the butterfly guard with an overhook and an underhook, there is a strong chance that he will attempt to get the upper hand by establishing double underhooks. In order for him to accomplish this, he must steal your underhook by swimming his arm underneath yours. Although the primary goal is for you to establish double underhooks so your sweeps become available, it is possible to use his aggressive movements against him by catching him in an omoplata. If he's attempting to swim his left arm underneath your right arm, begin by placing your right foot on his left hip and falling to your back to stretch him out and break his base. Then, in one fluid motion, swing your right leg over his left arm, pull your left leg out from underneath his body, and sit up into the omoplata position. I'm a huge fan of the omoplata from this position and all others because it's a tricky submission that can catch your opponent off guard.

I've secured the butterfly guard by establishing over-under control.

In an attempt to establish double underhooks, John pummels his left hand to the inside of my right arm.

I place my right foot on John's left hip.

BUTTERFLY GUARD

4 Driving my right foot into John's left hip, I fall to my back.

5 I drive off the mat with my left foot and begin wrapping my right leg around the outside of John's left shoulder.

6 I roll onto my left side and continue to wrap my right leg around the outside of John's left shoulder. Notice how I have his left arm trapped between my right leg and arm.

7 I slide my left leg out from underneath John's body and drive my right leg down into his left shoulder. Notice how I'm gripping the back of his left elbow with my right hand; this prevents him from freeing his left arm as I transition into the omoplata.

SUBMISSIONS 99

BUTTERFLY GUARD

8 Still applying downward pressure to John's left shoulder using my right leg, I post on my left hand, straighten out my left leg, and sit up.

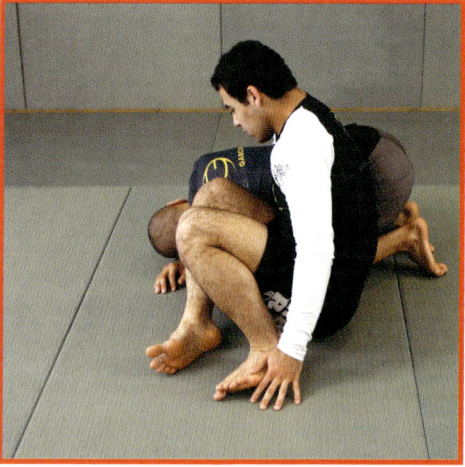

9 Pinching my knees together, I wrap my right leg around John's left arm, curl my left leg back toward my buttocks, and reach my right arm over his body.

10 I dig my right hand underneath John's right arm, drag my left arm across the right side of his face, and grip my hands together. To finish the omoplata, I drive his left shoulder into the mat using my right leg and pull his left forearm upwards by elevating my hips.

100 BUTTERFLY GUARD

MONOPLATA

This technique begins exactly as the last, but when you attempt to pull your leg out from underneath your opponent to sit up into the omoplata position, he counters by latching on to your leg. Although this prevents you from being able to finish the omoplata the traditional way, there is no need to abandon the submission. As you will see in the photos below, you can use your positioning to force your opponent onto his back and finish him from the mount position.

I've secured the butterfly guard by establishing over-under control.

In an attempt to establish double underhooks, John pummels his left hand to the inside of my right arm.

John manages to punch his left arm underneath my right armpit and wrap his arm around my back. As he does this, he drops his elevation and drives forward in an attempt to put my back on the mat.

BUTTERFLY GUARD

4

Instead of resisting John's forward momentum, I fall to my left side and place my right foot on his left hip.

5

I swing my right leg around the outside of John's left arm.

6

I wrap my right leg around John's left arm, plant my right foot on the mat on the left side of his head, and climb up to my left elbow. Notice how John is gripping my left leg with his right arm. This prevents me from pulling my left leg out from underneath his body and securing the omoplata submission. In order to continue to attack with the monoplata, I need to roll him to his back and work to finish the submission from the top position.

BUTTERFLY GUARD

BUTTERFLY GUARD

7 To roll John to his back, I push off the mat using my right foot and left arm, circle my hips in a counterclockwise direction into his left arm, and then post my right hand on the mat.

8 As John is forced to his back, I drop down to my right hip.

9 I grab the outside of my right knee with my left hand. Notice how John's left arm is trapped between my right leg and ribcage.

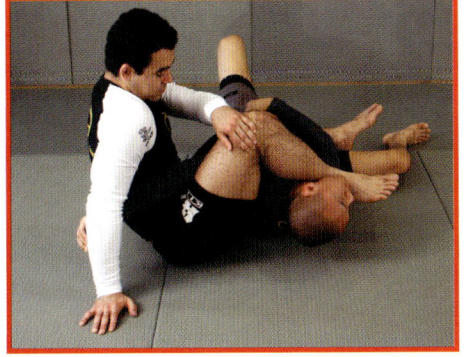

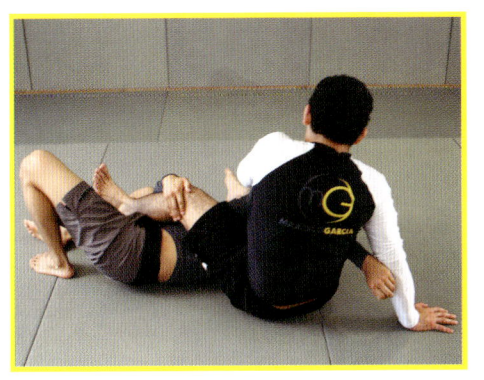

10 To finish the monoplata, I pull my left thigh into John's left elbow using my left hand.

BUTTERFLY GUARD   GI   NO-GI

GUILLOTINE CHOKE

If you exercise proper technique and timing, the guillotine choke is a quick and easy submission to obtain from the butterfly guard. In the sequence below, I demonstrate how to forcibly pull your opponent's head down to secure the choke. Although this can certainly work, the submission is best applied when your opponent drops his head low and drives forward.

1

John is down on his knees, looking for an opportunity to pass my guard.

2

I grab the back of John's head with my left hand.

3

Pulling down on John's head using my left hand, I wedge the inside of my right wrist underneath his throat.

104 BUTTERFLY GUARD

BUTTERFLY GUARD

4 Keeping the sharp part of my right forearm wedged underneath John's throat, I pull his head toward my lap using my left hand.

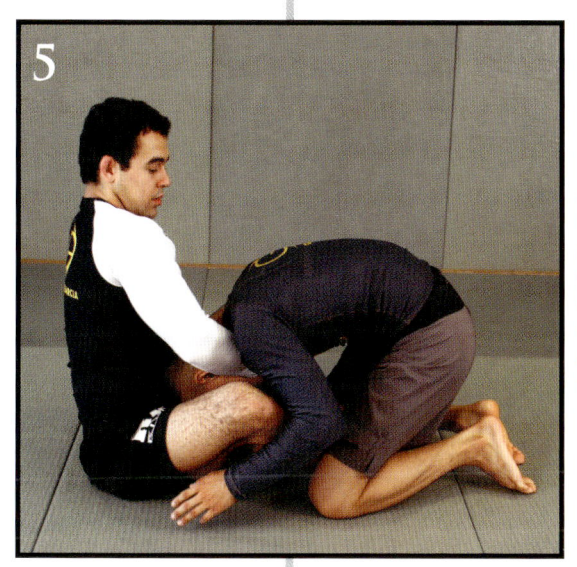

5 Now that I've pulled John's head into my lap, I straighten my back to trap his head in place, slip my left hand between the right side of his neck and shoulder, and then grab my right wrist with my left hand.

6 To finish the guillotine choke, I pinch my elbows tight to my sides, fold my chest over the back of John's head, and pull the inside of my right forearm into his throat using my left hand.

SUBMISSIONS 105

BUTTERFLY GUARD — GI — NO-GI

OFF BALANCE GUILLOTINE CHOKE SEQUENCE

In this sequence I demonstrate a more realistic scenario that might occur during a heated jiu-jitsu match when you're down on your butt and your opponent is posted on one knee and one foot. To set up the guillotine choke, force your opponent off balance by shoving him backward. On occasion you'll manage to shove your opponent all the way to his back, which allows you to assume the top position, but most of the time your opponent will recover from your shove and move back into you. As he comes forward to regain his balance, wrap up his neck as you did in the previous technique and fall to your side. Deciding which side to fall to should be based upon the positioning of your arms. If you have your right arm digging into your opponent's neck as I do in the photos below, you'll want to fall to your left side. Instead of stopping once you've dropped to your side, continue to roll across your shoulders and then come back up to your knees. Although this might seem strange, the roll allows you to sink the choke tighter without giving your opponent a chance to defend against the submission. Once you're back up on your knees, you then want to fall to your right side and squeeze the submission tight. The key to success with this technique is performing all of the steps in one fluid motion.

1 John is down on one knee in an attack-ready position, looking for an opening to pass my guard.

2 Before John can get his offense going, I place my right hand on his left knee, my left hand on his right shoulder, and push him backward.

3 To stop himself from falling backward, John posts his left hand on the mat.

106 BUTTERFLY GUARD

BUTTERFLY GUARD

4 To regain his balance and retaliate against my attack, John charges blindly forward into my guard. As he does this, I position the inside of my right forearm under his throat and reach my left hand around the back of his head.

5 As John continues to charge forward into my guard, I push down on his head with my left hand while keeping my right arm positioned underneath his neck.

6 As John progresses forward, I maneuver my left arm underneath his right arm, latch onto my right wrist with my left hand, and then climb up to my left foot and right knee.

SUBMISSIONS 107

BUTTERFLY GUARD

7

I halt John's forward progression by sprawling my hips back and folding my chest over his back.

8

In order to tighten up the guillotine, I need to drop to my left side, roll over my shoulders, climb back up to my knees, and then fall to my right side. To begin the process, I fall toward my left side.

9

Keeping my arms locked tight around John's neck, I roll onto my back.

108 BUTTERFLY GUARD

BUTTERFLY GUARD

10

As I roll onto my back, I post my feet on the mat as close to my butt as possible and then bridge over my right shoulder.

11

I roll over my right shoulder and climb up to my knees.

12

In one fluid motion, I draw both of my arms toward my torso, flare my left leg behind me, and slide my right leg underneath John's body.

SUBMISSIONS   109

BUTTERFLY GUARD

13

I begin falling toward my right side.

14

To finish the choke, I fall to my right side and pull on my right wrist with my left hand. Notice how I have elevated my left elbow. This gives me better leverage and maximizes my pulling power with my left hand, allowing me to drive my right wrist deep into John's throat.

THE X-GUARD

ESTABLISHING THE X-GUARD

The x-guard is not a defensive guard—it's a position that provides you with numerous options for sweeping your opponent or finishing the fight. In later sections I demonstrate many ways to accomplish both, but before you tackle your offensive options from the position, it is very important that you delve into this section and learn as many ways to establish the x-guard as possible. If you only learn how to set up the x-guard from the butterfly guard, you won't reach the position as nearly often as you would like. And there is nothing more frustrating than being unable to unleash your sweeps and submissions due to a lack of positioning. There is absolutely no reason for this to happen. As you will soon see, one of the best parts about the x-guard is that you can reach it from nearly every position. If you learn all of these routes, you'll become a dangerous competitor indeed.

SINGLE LEG TO X-GUARD SETUP

When up against a strong wrestler or an opponent with superior takedowns, it can be difficult to haul him from the standing position down to his back. If you don't feel like challenging his wrestling skills for fear of ending up in a compromising position, a good option is to utilize this technique to establish the x-guard, and then employ one of the moves from the next section to sweep your opponent to his back. With this particular technique, you want to shoot in on your opponent's lead leg, making the level change and penetration involved similar to that of a single leg takedown.

1

I'm standing an arm length away from Frank, preparing to unleash my attack.

2

I close the distance and move into Frank's comfort zone by dropping my elevation, stepping my right foot forward, and wrapping my right hand around the outside of his left knee. From here I can work to execute a single leg takedown, but not wanting to compete with Frank's takedown defense, I decide to use the control I have on his left leg to pull him into the x-guard.

3

I drop my left knee to the mat to lower my elevation.

THE X-GUARD

THE X-GUARD

ESTABLISHING THE X-GUARD

4

Posting on my left knee for balance, I place my right foot to the inside of Frank's left foot.

5

To gain control of Frank's right leg, I slide my left leg underneath my body, drop my left hip to the mat, and hook my left hand around the inside of his right hamstring.

6

In order to pull Frank into the x-guard, I need to position my body underneath his hips. To accomplish this, I roll onto my left shoulder, elevate his left foot off the mat by lifting my right foot into the air, draw his left leg over my body using the strength in my right leg, and rotate in a clockwise direction by pulling on his right leg using my left underhook. It is important to notice how I keep my right leg bent at a ninety-degree angle while also keeping my right hand locked around the outside of his left knee. The former gives me the leverage I need to pull his left leg off the mat, and the latter prevents him from stepping his left leg over my right hook, freeing his leg, and passing into a dominant position.

ESTABLISHING THE X-GUARD

THE X-GUARD

7

In an attempt to maintain his balance, Frank drops his left foot to the mat.

8

The instant Frank drops his left foot to the mat, I maneuver my left foot to the front of his left thigh. It's important to notice how I keep my right hand planted on his right knee, as well as how I'm continuing to control his right leg using my left underhook. As a rule of thumb, you always want to keep your right hand glued to your opponent's thigh until you've secured your second hook and established the x-guard position.

9

To establish the x-guard position, I stretch out both legs, pull Frank's right leg over my left shoulder, and then clasp my hands over the top of his right knee and thigh to prevent him from pulling his leg out and escaping the position. To hinder him from breaking free of my hooks and advancing into a dominant position, I keep both of my legs tense.

GI NO-GI THE X-GUARD

PULLING THE X-GUARD FROM STANDING

If you're competing in a Brazilian Jiu-Jitsu match, this technique is an excellent way to pull your opponent directly into the x-guard from the stand-up position. However, to make a fluid transition into the x-guard using this technique, you first have to grip one of your opponent's sleeves with both hands. Once you've established a strong grip, place your foot on his hip. If you grabbed his right sleeve, place your left foot on his right hip. If you grabbed his left sleeve, place your right foot on his left hip. Obtaining this control allows you to push and pull on your opponent at the same time, which stretches him out and prevents him from dropping from the standing position to the mat as you fall to your back. The goal is to keep him stretched out long enough to gain control of his leg, secure both hooks, and establish the x-guard. If you fail to secure the x-guard before your opponent recovers his base and drops to the mat, you not only lose your opportunity to secure the x-guard, but you also risk having your opponent pass your guard into a dominant position.

1 I'm standing in front of Babs, searching for an opening to attack.

2 Although I could attempt to claim the top position by wrestling Babs to the mat, I decide instead to pull him directly into the x-guard, which will allow me to sweep him over to his back. To begin the x-guard setup, I grab his right wrist with my left hand.

3 Maintaining a solid grip on Babs' right wrist with my left hand, I grab the excess cloth of his right sleeve between my right thumb and index finger.

ESTABLISHING THE X-GUARD   115

THE X-GUARD

4

To secure a solid grip on Babs' right sleeve, I make a fist with my right hand and pull my right elbow into my body. As I do this, I reposition my left hand by wrapping my fingers underneath his right wrist. Notice how my left palm is now facing upward.

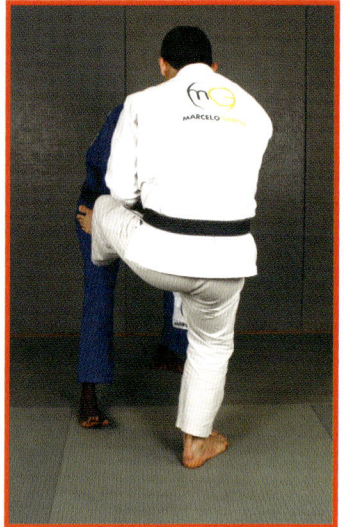

5

I pull Babs' right arm toward my body using both hands and place my left foot on his right hip.

6

Maintaining control of Babs' right arm using both hands, I keep my left foot planted on his right hip and fall to my back. As I land, I immediately drive my foot into his hip and pull down on his right arm using both hands. Not only does this keep him in the standing position, but it also breaks his posture, which makes it difficult for him to escape the position. It is important to notice that instead of falling straight back, I've fallen slightly to my left. This gives me the angle I need to gain control of Babs' right leg.

THE X-GUARD

7

To secure control over Babs' right leg, I release my left grip on his right wrist and grab the back of his right foot. Notice how I wrap my fingers around his Achilles tendon.

8

Continuing to drive my left foot into Babs' right hip, I pull his right foot off the mat using my left hand.

9

Maintaining a strong grip on Babs' right sleeve using my right hand, I move my right leg to the inside of his left leg and then hook my foot around the back of his knee. As I do this, I release my left grip on his right foot and maneuver my left hand to the inside of his right leg.

ESTABLISHING THE X-GUARD

THE X-GUARD

10

Still controlling Babs' right arm with my right hand, I wrap my left arm around the back of his right leg and clasp my left hand over his knee.

11

To secure the x-guard, I release my right grip on Babs' right sleeve, stretch out both of my legs, and wrap my right wrist over the top of his right knee. From here, it is important to keep your hands locked tight around your opponent's right leg to prevent him from pulling his leg out and escaping the position. You also want to keep both of your legs tense to hinder him from escaping your hooks and advancing into a dominant position.

DOUBLE KNEE CONTROL TO X-GUARD

This is another technique that you can utilize when you don't wish to contend with your opponent's takedowns. Instead of standing up with him and operating in his area of strength, you drop your butt to the mat, scoot toward his legs, and wrap him up in the x-guard while he is still standing. The most important aspect is timing and speed. Your opponent won't just stand there and allow you to work slowly through your x-guard setup. He will do everything in his power to pass your guard and secure top control. To prevent him from stepping his free leg over your body during your setup, it is crucial that you control both of his legs using your hands until you can establish your second hook.

Frank is on his feet, looking for an opening to pass my guard.

I extend both legs straight out so that my feet are positioned between Frank's legs.

To close the distance on Frank, I drive my heels into the mat, curl both legs inward, and scoot my butt toward my feet. As I draw close, I cup both hands around the outside of his legs, gripping the tendons that run down the side of his knees.

THE X-GUARD

4

Dropping back toward my left side, I hook my right instep around the back of Frank's left knee and pull his left leg toward me using my right hand. These last two actions force him to take a small step forward with his left foot.

5

In order to position my body underneath Frank and secure the x-guard, I need to force him to step his left leg over my body. To begin this transition, I roll to my back, push off the mat with my left foot, and rotate my body in a clockwise direction. At the same time, I use the momentum of my roll along with the strength of my right leg to pull Frank's left foot off the mat and draw his left leg over my body. Notice how my right leg is bent at an angle, and how I keep my right hand locked around the outside of his left knee. The former allows me to draw his left leg off the mat, and the latter prevents him from stepping over my right hook, freeing his leg, and passing into a dominant position.

6

As Frank's left foot hits the mat, I wrap my left arm around the back of his right leg and cup my left hand around his thigh just above the knee.

THE X-GUARD

THE X-GUARD

ESTABLISHING THE X-GUARD

7 Keeping my right hand pinned to Frank's left leg, I maneuver my left leg to the inside of his left thigh.

8 Now that I have established my second hook, I release my right grip on Frank's left leg, hook my right arm over the top of his right leg, and grip the outside of his right calf using my right hand. Notice how I've positioned my right hand just below my left.

9 To secure the x-guard position, I turn my shoulders in a clockwise direction, draw Frank's right leg over my left shoulder using my arms, and straighten my legs. Every time you land in the x-guard, it is important to keep your legs tense and your opponent's base stretched out as much as possible. Not only does this make it easier for you to sweep your opponent, but it will also prevent him from escaping your guard.

ESTABLISHING THE X-GUARD 121

SINGLE LEG ATTACK FROM THE BOTTOM POSITION

When I fought Renzo Gracie in Abu Dhabi World Championships, I used this exact technique to setup the x-guard. I was sitting on my butt, and he was posted on one knee and one foot. I knew he was looking for an opportunity to pass my guard, but instead of waiting for him to make his move, I immediately secured control of his lead leg using both hands, forced his leg over my shoulder, and then established my hooks and secured the x-guard. Once I had the position, I swept him over to his back and obtained dominant control, which resulted in me winning the match. If I had hesitated for even a moment, my chance to secure the x-guard would have passed me by and the outcome of the fight might have been different. As I mentioned in the book's introduction, believing in the x-guard and having confidence in your ability to sweep your opponent from the position is vital. If you don't have that confidence, the commitment won't be there. And without commitment, the x-guard system is not effective.

1 Babs' is down on one knee and one foot, looking for an opening to pass my guard.

2 To make a smooth transition into the x-guard, I need to close the distance between Babs and I before he initiates an attack. I begin the process by extending both of my legs so that my feet are positioned between his legs.

3 Driving my heels into the mat, I curl both legs inward and scoot my butt toward my feet. As I close the gap between our bodies, I reach my right hand over the top of Babs' right leg, maneuver my left hand underneath his right thigh, and then clasp my left hand over my right hand just above his knee on the outside of his right thigh. It is important to make this transition as quickly as possible. If you hesitate for even a moment, your opponent will have the time he needs to mount a defense and stop your transition.

THE X-GUARD

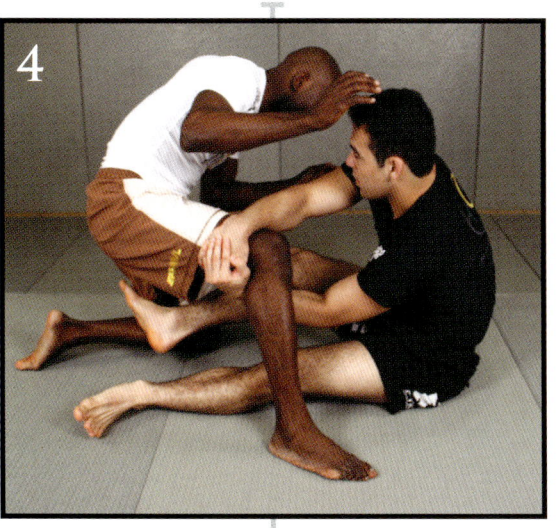

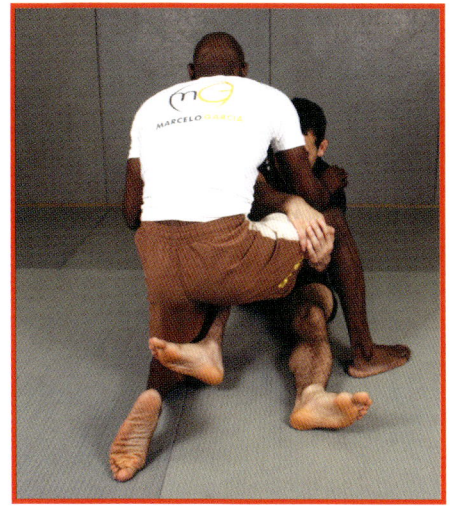

ESTABLISHING THE X-GUARD

4

I straighten out my left leg, as well as hook my right foot behind Babs' left thigh.

5

Keeping my right instep hooked around the inside of Babs' left thigh, I roll to my back and pull his right leg over my left shoulder using both hands.

6

The instant I come down onto my back, I drive my left foot straight into the air so that the bottom of my foot is facing the ceiling.

ESTABLISHING THE X-GUARD

THE X-GUARD

7

To create the space I need to secure my top hook, I drive my straightened left leg toward the mat, and then use the momentum of the downward kick to sit upright.

8

Having created space with my previous actions, I maneuver my left foot to the inside of Babs' left hip.

9

Maintaining tight control of Babs' left leg, I fall to my back and secure the x-guard position.

COLLAR AND SLEEVE CONTROL TO X-GUARD

This technique is utilized in the same scenario as the last—you're sitting on your butt, and your opponent is posted on one knee and one foot in the attack position. Instead of grabbing his posted foot with both hands as you did in the previous move, you're going to setup the x-guard by latching on to his sleeve and collar. If you can manage the grips, I would recommend using this technique rather than the previous one because you have a lot more control over your opponent's body. If you're an MMA fighter or submission grappler, the no-gi version of this technique is covered next.

1

Frank is down on his left knee and right foot, looking for an opening to pass my guard.

2

The first step in this technique is to close the distance between my opponent and me and gain control of his upper body. To begin the process, I extend my legs so that my feet are between Frank's legs. At the same time, I grip the inside of his left collar with my right hand and grip the bottom of his right sleeve with my left hand.

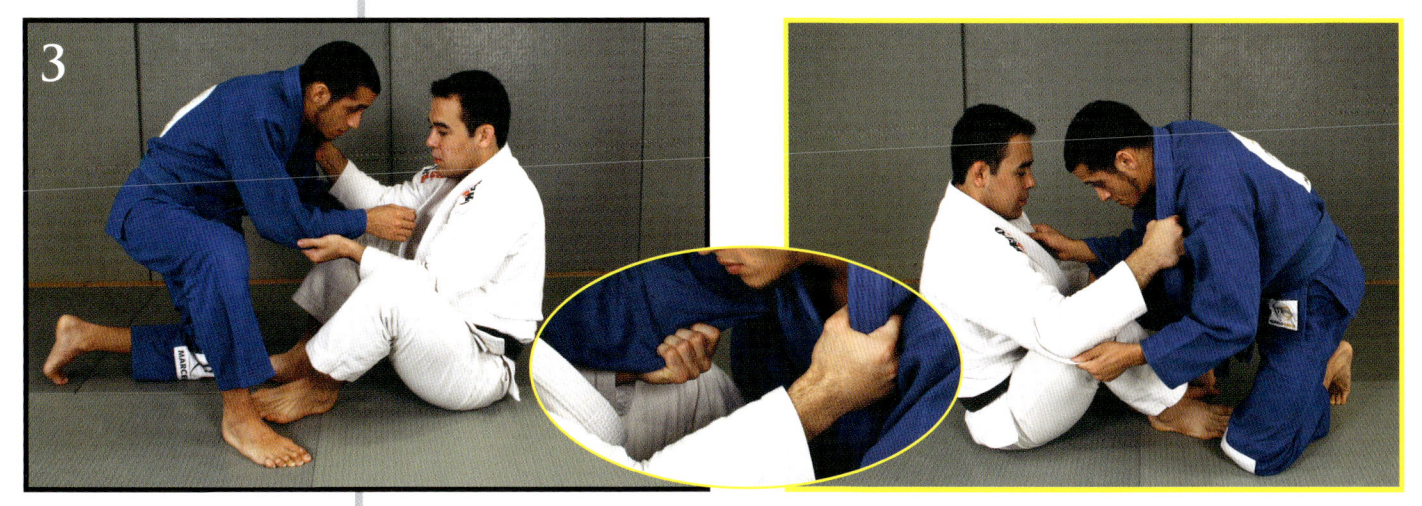

3

To close the distance between Frank and me, I drive my heels into the mat, coil both legs inward, and scoot my butt toward my feet. At the same time, I pull Frank's upper body toward me using my grip on his sleeve and collar.

ESTABLISHING THE X-GUARD   125

THE X-GUARD

4 Still pulling Frank's upper body toward me using my sleeve and collar control, I drop back and hook both of my feet under his right thigh.

5 Continuing to pull on Frank's sleeve and collar, I roll all the way to my back and use both of my legs to heft his right leg off the mat.

6 Now that I've moved Frank's right leg over my hips, I straighten out my left leg, coil my right leg inward, and allow Frank's right leg to drop down on top of my right shin. Once accomplished, I hook my left arm around the outside of his right leg and cup my wrist just above his knee.

126 THE X-GUARD

THE X-GUARD

7

To create the space I need to secure my second hook, I drive my straightened left leg toward the mat and then use the momentum I created with the downward kick to sit upright. It is important to notice that I'm still using my left arm to control his right leg, and I still have a solid grip on his left collar. The former prevents him from freeing his leg and escaping the position, and the latter provides balance and gives me control of his upper body.

8

To secure my top hook, I maneuver my left leg over the top of my right leg and then slip my left foot to the inside of Frank's left thigh.

9

To secure the x-guard position, I roll to my back, release my right grip on Frank's left collar, and cup my right hand over his right thigh just above his knee.

ESTABLISHING THE X-GUARD 127

HEAD AND WRIST CONTROL TO X-GUARD

This technique is the no-gi version of the previous move. All the steps are essentially the same, but because you don't have a collar and sleeve to latch on to, you set up the x-guard using neck and wrist control. Other than your grips, the only thing you need to change is the speed at which you execute the technique. Grabbing your opponent's head and wrist doesn't provide very tight control, and to prevent your opponent from escaping the x-guard and obtaining a more dominant position, you want to move through the steps as quickly as possible. The instant you grab his neck and lock up his wrist, you want to begin your transition.

1

Babs is down on his left knee and right foot, looking for an opportunity to pass my guard.

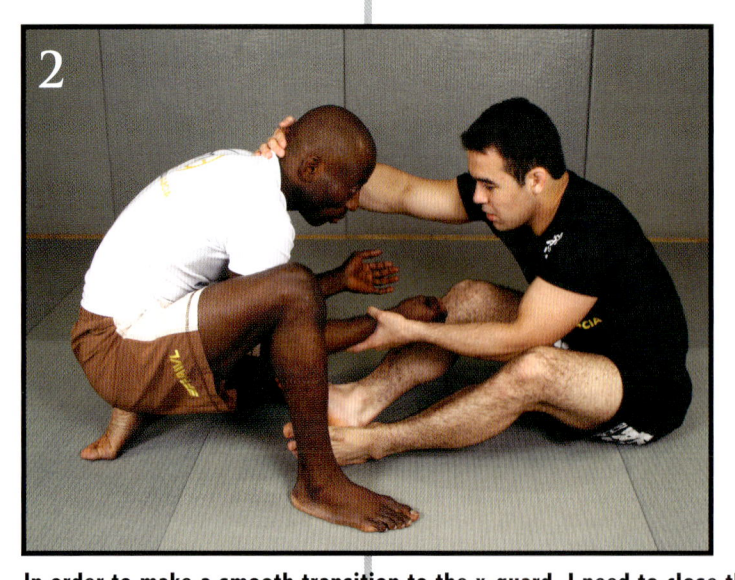

2

In order to make a smooth transition to the x-guard, I need to close the distance between Babs and me as quickly as possible. To begin the process, I extend both of my legs so that my feet are between his legs. At the same time, I grab his right wrist with my left hand and cup my right wrist around the back of his neck.

128 THE X-GUARD

THE X-GUARD

3

I use the head and wrist control I established to prevent Babs from disengaging, as well as help pull my body towards his. At the same time, I drive my heels into the mat, curl both legs inward, and scoot my butt toward my feet.

4

I reposition both feet so that they are directly underneath Babs' right leg.

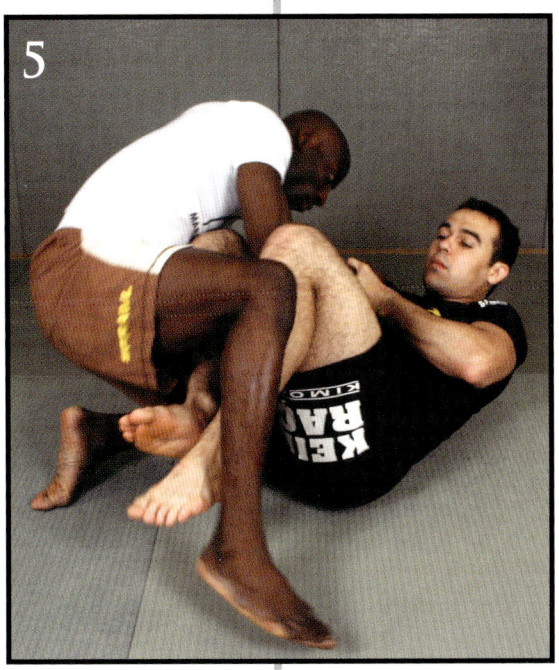

5

Using my right hand to pull down on Babs' head, I roll to my back and hook both feet underneath his right thigh.

ESTABLISHING THE X-GUARD

THE X-GUARD

6

Using the momentum of my backward roll, I elevate both of my legs into the air to heft Babs' right leg off the mat. When executing this step, it is important to keep both of your legs bent at a slight angle to prevent your opponent from slipping his leg over the top of your hooks and falling into the mount position.

7

Now that I have moved Babs' right leg over my hips, I straighten out my left leg, coil my right leg inward, and allow his right leg to drop on top of my right shin. Once accomplished, I release my left grip on his right wrist and begin sliding my left arm underneath his right leg.

8

Keeping Babs' posture broken by applying downward pressure on his head using my right hand, I wrap my left arm around the outside of his right leg and then use that control to position his leg over my left shoulder.

THE X-GUARD

9

I drive my straightened left leg toward the mat and then use the momentum of the downward kick to sit upright. It is important to notice that I'm still controlling Babs' right leg using my left arm, and I still have my right hand hooked around the back of his head. The former prevents him from freeing his leg and escaping the position, and the latter gives me better control over his upper body.

10

Sliding my left leg over the top of my right leg, I secure my top hook by placing my left foot to the inside of Babs' left hip.

11

To secure the x-guard position, I keep both of my hooks intact, roll to my back, remove my right hand from the back of Babs' head, and then hook my right wrist around his right hamstring.

ESTABLISHING THE X-GUARD

CROSS GRIP SLEEVE CONTROL TO X-GUARD

In this scenario, you're sitting on your butt and your opponent is posted on one knee and one foot. Instead of gaining control of his collar and sleeve as you did in previous techniques, you double up on one of his arms by grabbing it with both of your hands. If you're able to secure this form of control, pulling on his arm offsets his base, making for a fairly easy transition into the x-guard. Instead of having to lift his entire weight to get his leg up to your shoulder, which is the method you've used up to this point, you only have to lift one of his legs due to his off-centered base. If you look at the photos below, you'll see that this can be accomplished using one leg instead of two. To learn how to execute the no-gi version of this technique, see the next sequence in this section.

Frank is posted on his left knee and right foot, looking for an opening to pass my guard. Notice how my elbows are to the inside of my legs and my hands are out in front of me. Not only does this positioning allow me to attack, but it also allows me to defend should Frank reach for my legs or attempt to latch on to my collar or sleeve.

In order to make a smooth transition to the x-guard, I first have to establish control of one of Frank's arms by gripping his sleeve. To begin this process, I grab his right wrist with my left hand.

3

Still controlling Frank's right wrist with my left hand, I pinch the loose cloth at the edge of his right sleeve between my right index finger and thumb, and then wrap my other fingers around the raised fabric. This allows me to gain control of his arm by using just his sleeve.

4

Now that I have a firm grip on Frank's right sleeve with my right hand, I extend both legs so that my feet are positioned between his legs. As I do this, I release my left grip on his right wrist.

5

To close the distance, I drive my heels into the mat, curl my legs inward, and scoot my butt toward my feet. As I do this, I pull Frank's right arm into me using my right hand, grab his right triceps with my left hand, and then use both of my grips to move his right arm toward his left side.

ESTABLISHING THE X-GUARD

6

Keeping Frank's right arm on his left side using my grips, I straighten out my left leg so that it is positioned to the inside of his right foot.

7

Continuing to pull Frank's right arm to the left side of his body, I hook my right foot underneath his right hamstring.

8

Still pulling Frank's right arm to his left side, I roll to my back to generate the momentum needed to lift his right leg off the mat using my right leg. Because I have him stretched out, I only have to use one leg to draw his hooked leg over my body. If you don't have your opponent's base broken down in this manner, you'll have to use both legs as demonstrated in the previous technique.

THE X-GUARD

9

As I move Frank's right leg over my hips, I reach my right arm over the top of his right leg and grab the back of his right calf. At the same time, I hook my left arm underneath his right leg and coil my left wrist around the back of his calf.

10

Dropping to my back, I use both of my hands to pull Frank's right leg over my left shoulder. As I do this, I move my right hook underneath his left leg so that my right instep is pressed against his left hamstring.

11

Now that I've established proper control of Frank's right leg, I need to create enough space to slip my left hook to the inside of his left thigh. To begin the process, I elevate my left foot toward the ceiling and prepare to kick my leg to the mat to generate enough momentum to sit upright.

ESTABLISHING THE X-GUARD 135

THE X-GUARD

12

I drive my left leg to the mat and use the momentum to sit upright.

13

I secure my top hook by placing my left leg over the top of my right leg and then slipping my left foot to the inside of Frank's left hip.

14

Maintaining tight control of Frank's right leg using my hands, I drop to my back and secure the x-guard position.

CROSS GRIP TO ARM DRAG X-GUARD SETUP

The cross grip to arm drag x-guard setup is similar to the previous technique, but you have to make a few no-gi modifications. The first adjustment is the control. Since your opponent doesn't have a sleeve to latch on to, you want to grab ahold of his far wrist and then utilize an arm drag to offset his base. The second difference is how you establish control of his leg. Instead of using both hands to bring his leg over your shoulder, you only use one. The reason you can use both hands when grappling with a gi is because you're able to really stretch your opponent out and offset his base with sleeve control. This allows you to not only let go of his arm completely, but also lift his posted leg using just one of your legs. When you don't have a sleeve to latch on to, it's more difficult to stretch your opponent out, you can't completely release his captured arm because he might escape the x-guard and obtain a dominant position, and you need to lift his leg up to your shoulder using both of your legs because his weight is less off-centered. It's certainly not as easy of a technique to execute without a gi, but as long as you underhook your opponent's posted leg with your near arm, maintain control of his isolated arm with your opposite hand, and use both of your legs to heft his leg over your shoulder, you'll be in excellent position to secure both of your hooks and establish the x-guard position.

Babs is posting on his left knee and right foot, looking for an opening to pass my guard. Notice how my elbows are to the inside of my legs and my hands are out in front of me. Not only does this allow me to attack, but it also allows me to defend should Babs reach for my legs or attempt to latch on to my head or wrist.

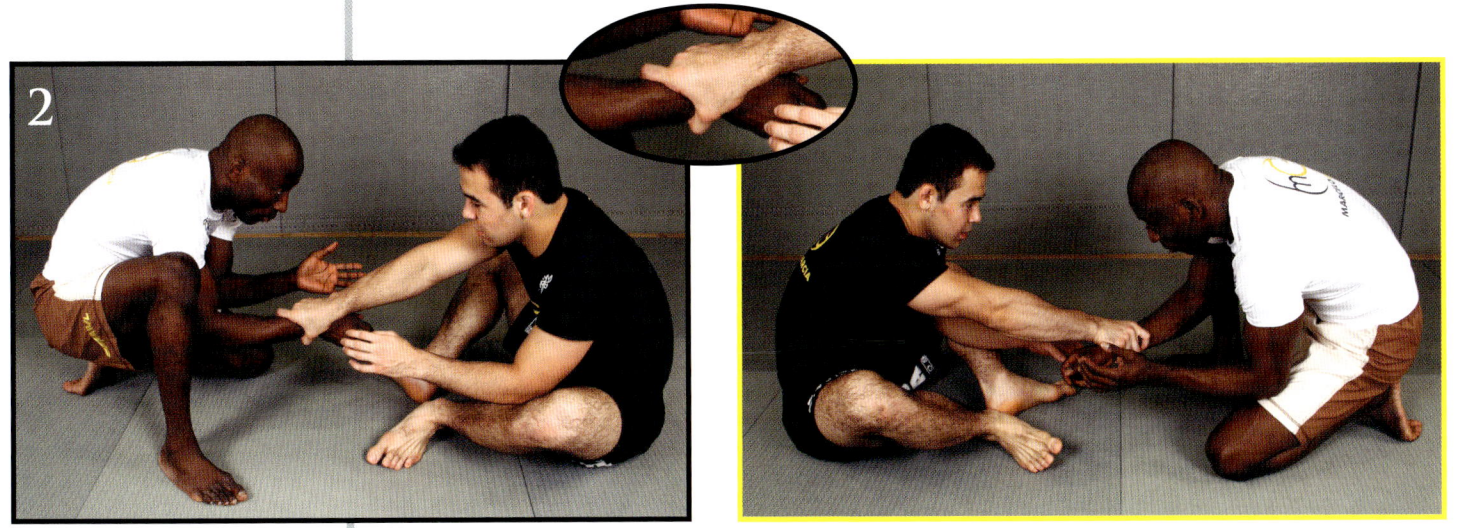

Before Babs can initiate an attack, I reach my right hand across my body and latch on to his right wrist. Notice that my right palm is facing the mat.

THE X-GUARD

3

Pulling Babs' right arm away from his body using my right hand, I grip the back of his triceps with my left hand and extend both legs so that my feet are positioned between his legs.

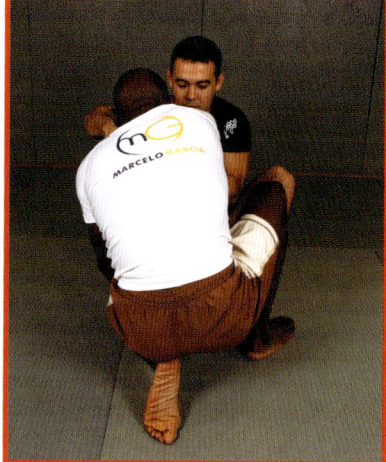

4

To close the distance, I drive my heels into the mat, curl my legs inward, and scoot my butt toward my feet. At the same time, I force Babs' right arm to the left side of his body by pulling on his wrist with my right hand and pushing on his right elbow with my left triceps tie.

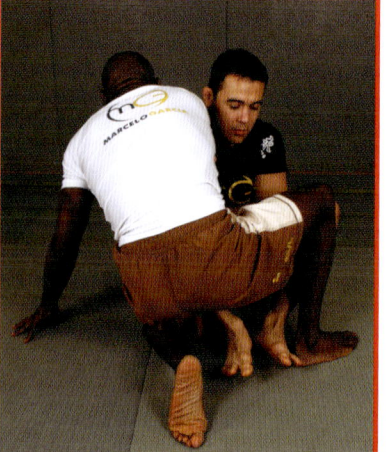

5

As I move into Babs' comfort zone, I release my right grip on his right wrist, move my right hand to the inside of his right arm so my thumb is in his armpit, and wrap my fingers around is triceps. Accomplishing this puts me in the arm drag position, and I instantly place both feet directly underneath Babs' right leg and prepare to roll to my back.

138 THE X-GUARD

THE X-GUARD

6

In one fluid motion, I drag Babs' right arm toward the left side of his body using my right hand, roll to my back, and hook both feet underneath his right hamstring.

7

As I roll onto my back, I lift Babs' right leg off the mat by elevating both of my legs toward the ceiling.

8

Having maneuvered Babs' right leg over the top of my hips, I straighten my left leg upward and coil my right leg toward my body. Notice how this causes his right leg to fall on top of my right shin. As this occurs, I hook my left arm around the back of his right leg, cupping my hand around his thigh just above his knee.

ESTABLISHING THE X-GUARD

THE X-GUARD

9

Now that I've secured control of Babs' right leg using my left arm, I need to create enough space to slip my left hook to the inside of his left thigh. To begin the process, I draw my straightened left leg toward my head.

10

I drive my left leg toward the mat and then use the generated momentum to sit upright. Notice how I maintain control of his right leg using my left arm, as well as maintain a strong grip on his right arm using my right hand. The former prevents him from freeing his leg and escaping the position and the latter gives me slight control over his upper body.

11

I move my left leg over the top of my right leg. Next, I secure my top hook by slipping my left foot to the inside of Babs' left hip.

140 THE X-GUARD

12

As soon as I establish both hooks, I release my right grip on Babs' right arm and then hook my right wrist over his right knee. Notice how I've placed my right hand just above my left.

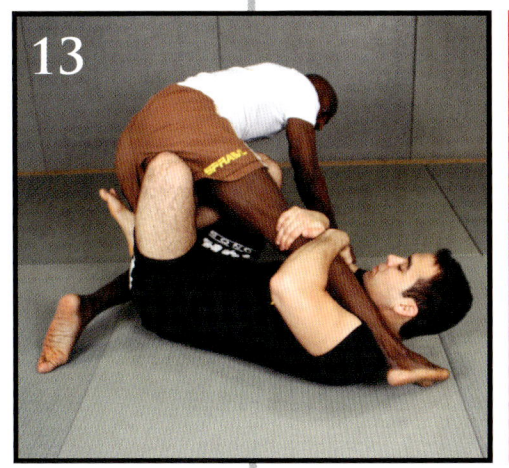

13

To secure the x-guard position, I keep both hooks intact, maintain solid control of Babs' right leg using my hands, and fall to my back.

ESTABLISHING THE X-GUARD

DOUBLE ELBOW CONTROL TO X-GUARD

When I'm on my butt and my opponent is on both of his knees, a lot of the time he will attempt to grab my legs or ankles in an effort to pass my guard. To prevent him from achieving his goal, I'll continuously block his grips using my hands. In reaction to my counters, my opponent will often bring his arms in tight to his body and wait for the right time to attack. Although his tight posture makes it difficult for me to get a solid grip that I would normally apply in order to transition into the x-guard, I still have a very effective option. As he draws his arms in tight, I'll close the distance between us as quickly as possible and take advantage of his tight positioning by grabbing the outside of his elbows. The instant I get this control, he can no longer attack or grab my legs, which allows me to force the butterfly guard, roll back, lift his body off the mat using my legs, and then use the space and momentum I created to transition into the x-guard. It's an excellent technique to utilize for both gi and no-gi practitioners.

Frank is down on his knees, looking for an opening to pass my guard. Notice how both of my elbows are positioned to the inside of my legs and my hands are out in front of me. Not only does this allow me to attack, but it also allows me to defend should Frank reach for my legs or attempt to control my collar or sleeve.

From this position, my primary goal is to close the distance before Frank can mount an attack. I begin the process by straightening both legs so that my feet are between his legs. Notice how Frank has kept his elbows tight to his body. Paying attention to your opponent's arm positioning is very important because it will dictate the type of control you need to utilize as you move into his comfort zone. In this situation, I will use double elbow control to take advantage of Frank's tight posture.

THE X-GUARD

3

To close the distance, I drive my heels into the mat, curl both legs inward, and scoot my butt toward my feet. As I do this, I reach both arms out, grab the outside of Frank's elbows with my hands, and pinch his arms together. The idea is to temporarily immobilize your opponent so you can get both of your feet underneath his legs, close the gap between your bodies, and establish the butterfly guard position. If you don't immobilize your opponent by pinching his arms together, he'll have time to back out or reach down and mess with your feet as you make the transition.

4

Still pinching Frank's arms together, I straighten both legs again, position my feet directly underneath his hips, and prepare to move into his comfort zone.

5

I dig both of my heels into the mat, curl my legs inward, and scoot my butt toward my feet. Now that I've closed the distance, I establish the butterfly guard position by hooking both feet underneath Frank's hips.

ESTABLISHING THE X-GUARD   143

THE X-GUARD

6

As soon as I establish the butterfly guard position, I roll to my back and use both of my legs to elevate Frank's hips off the mat. When doing this, it is important to keep both of your legs tense and use the backward momentum of the roll to help lift your opponent's body.

7

As I lift Frank's hips off the mat, I straighten my left leg upward and coil my right heel toward my buttocks. As his left leg drops down on top of my right leg, I keep my instep pressed against his thigh. This positioning will serve as my bottom hook as I transition into the x-guard.

8

As Frank's right leg slides down my straightened left leg, I release my left grip on his right elbow, underhook his right leg with my left arm, and then maneuver his right leg over my left shoulder. At the same time, I draw my straightened left leg toward my head.

THE X-GUARD

9

To create the space I need to secure my top hook, I drive my left leg toward the mat and then use the momentum to sit upright.

10

To secure my top hook, I place my left leg over the top of my right leg and then slip my left foot to the inside of Frank's left thigh.

11

Maintaining tight control of Frank's left leg using my hooks, I establish the x-guard by falling to my back and cupping my right hand around the back of his right calf.

ESTABLISHING THE X-GUARD 145

THE X-GUARD   GI   NO-GI

DOUBLE UNDER-HOOK CONTROL TO X-GUARD

As I mentioned in the previous technique, a lot of the time when you're sitting on your butt and your opponent is on his knees, he will draw his arms in tight to his body to prevent you from gaining control of his wrist or arms. In such a scenario, it's best to quickly close the distance, gain control of his elbows, and set up the x-guard using the previous technique. However, sometimes your opponent will pull his arms in tight to his body and purposely flare his elbows out to hinder you from gaining control of his elbows. In such a situation, closing the distance, shooting your arms underneath his arms to establish underhooks, and then transitioning to the x-guard is an excellent option. A lot of times your opponent will simply forget that you can set up the x-guard off the underhooks, but once you make your move, the chances are he will remember in a hurry. The faster you get your hooks, the more success you will have. If your opponent pulls his arms back into his body before you can secure the underhooks, your best option is to switch gears and set up the x-guard by latching on to his elbows and utilizing the previous technique.

1

Frank is down on both knees, looking for an opening to pass my guard. Notice how my elbows are to the inside of my legs and my hands are out in front of me. Not only does this allow me to attack, but it also allows me to defend should he reach for my legs or attempt to gain control of my collar or sleeve.

2

To begin closing the distance between Frank and me, I straighten my legs so that my feet are positioned between his legs. Notice how Frank's elbows are flared out to his sides. As I mentioned in the previous technique, it is important to pay attention to your opponent's arm positioning because it will dictate the type of control you need to utilize. Because both of my opponent's arms are flared out to his sides, I will work for double underhooks. If he was pinching his elbows tight to his body, I would use double elbow control as I did in the last technique.

THE X-GUARD

3

I reach both of my arms straight out and dive my hands underneath Frank's arms.

4

To close the distance and secure the butterfly guard position, I drive my heels into the mat, curl my legs inward, and scoot my butt toward my feet. At the same time, I secure double underhook control by digging both of my arms underneath Frank's arms and then pulling my body into his.

5

Controlling Frank's upper body with my underhooks, I roll to my back and use both of my legs to elevate his hips off the mat. It is important to mention that I'm keeping my legs tense and using the backward momentum of the roll to help lift his body.

ESTABLISHING THE X-GUARD 147

THE X-GUARD

6

As I lift Frank's hips off the mat, I straighten my left leg upward and coil my right heel toward my buttocks. As his right leg drops down on top of my right leg, I keep my instep pressed against his thigh. This positioning will serve as my bottom hook as I transition into the x-guard.

7

In order to establish control of Frank's right leg, I need to offset his base by pushing his weight to my right side. I accomplish this by lowering my left leg toward the mat, and then placing my left hand in Frank's right armpit and pushing his body to my right side.

8

As soon as I push Frank's upper body to my side, I underhook his right leg with my left hand and wrap my right arm over the top of his right leg.

THE X-GUARD

9

I use my hands to move Frank's right leg over my left shoulder, and then I kick my left leg toward the mat to generate the momentum I need to sit upright.

10

Having created space by sitting up, I place my left leg over the top of my right leg and then slip my left foot to the inside of Frank's left thigh.

11

Using both arms to maintain control of Frank's right leg, I roll to my back and secure the x-guard position.

ESTABLISHING THE X-GUARD

FULL GUARD TO X-GUARD

As I'm sure you know, there are jiu-jitsu players out there who are absolute masters at passing the guard. If you're up against such an opponent and are hesitant to open your guard for fear he will pass into a more dominant position, a good option is to utilize this x-guard setup from full guard. The technique works best when grappling with a gi because you can secure a tight grip on your opponent's sleeve, which allows you to maneuver his arm into a position that nullifies his passes as you set up the x-guard. If you fail to obtain a tight grip on his sleeve and attempt to execute this technique, you not only run the risk of having your opponent shut down your transition by grabbing your lapel, but you also run the risk of having him pass your guard and obtaining a more dominant position.

1

I've got Babs locked in my closed guard.

2

I pinch the cloth on Babs' right sleeve using my right index finger and thumb and pull it away from his wrist. Next, I grip the raised fabric using my other fingers. By grabbing his sleeve in this manner, I have just gained control of his wrist.

3

I move Babs' right arm toward the left side of his body by pulling on his sleeve with my right hand and pushing on his right wrist with my left hand. It is important to note that you can use this same technique to break your opponent's grip when he is latching on to your collar.

THE X-GUARD

ESTABLISHING THE X-GUARD

4 — Using my right grip and left hand, I force Babs' right arm all the way to the left side of his body.

5 — Now that Babs' right arm is on the left side of his body, I grab his right triceps with my left hand to increase my control of his arm.

6 — Still controlling Babs' right arm with both hands, I unhook my feet and open my guard.

7 — Continuing to control Babs' right arm with both hands, I step my left leg over his right leg and then hook my left foot around the inside of his right instep. Once I establish this hook, I can use it to stretch out Babs' base and create the space I need to secure a butterfly hook on his right leg.

ESTABLISHING THE X-GUARD 151

THE X-GUARD

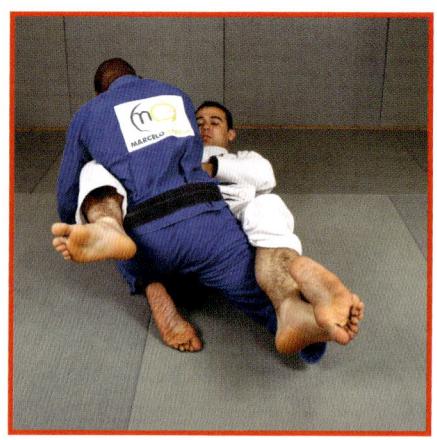

8

Keeping the toes of my left foot flexed toward the ceiling, I force Babs' right leg backward by stretching out my left leg.

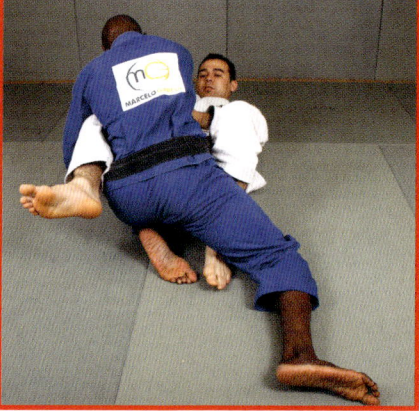

9

Now that I have stretched out Babs' right leg, I unhook my left foot from around the inside of his right instep and quickly maneuver it to the inside of his right hip. It is important that you make this transition before your opponent has a chance to pull his right knee back underneath his body and reestablish his base.

10

Still controlling Babs' right arm using both hands, I use the left butterfly hook I established to lift his right leg off the mat.

11

I straighten my left leg toward the ceiling, forcing Babs' right leg to fall toward my left side. As I do this, I release my grip on his triceps and hook my left arm underneath his right leg.

152 THE X-GUARD

THE X-GUARD

ESTABLISHING THE X-GUARD

13 I hook my left arm around Babs' right leg and then use that control to pull his leg over my left shoulder. Notice how I am still keeping his right arm on the left side of his body using my right grip on his sleeve. This prevents him from posturing up and reestablishing his base, which would make transitioning to the x-guard difficult to manage.

14 I kick my elevated left leg toward the mat, straighten out my right leg, and sit up.

15 I secure my bottom hook by wrapping my right foot around the back of Babs' left knee. To secure my top hook, I bring my left leg over my right and then wrap my left foot around the front of Babs' left thigh. It is very important not release control of your opponent's right sleeve before you get both of your hooks and establish the x-guard.

16 To secure the x-guard, I drop to my back, release my control of Babs' right arm, and wrap my right arm over his right leg.

ESTABLISHING THE X-GUARD 153

FULL GUARD TO X-GUARD (OPPONENT STANDING)

In the previous technique I demonstrated how to set up the x-guard from the full guard when your opponent is down on both knees. Here I show how to set up the x-guard from the full guard when your opponent climbs to his feet and attempts to break open your legs from the standing position. In order to make the transition, the first thing you need to do is pick a side. Deciding which side to pick boils down to what feels more comfortable and natural. In the beginning, it's not important to master setting up the x-guard from both sides. That should come after you've mastered the various setups, sweeps, and submissions from the side that you naturally go to. Once you've chosen a side, the next step in this technique is to rip your opponent's hand off your lapel so that you control his arm. Moving his arm across your body allows you to gain control of his leg, place both feet on his hips, and push his weight back to create enough space to establish your hooks and form the x-guard. If you desire to learn this technique no-gi, see the next technique in this section.

I've got Frank locked in my closed guard. Notice how he is gripping my lapel with both hands.

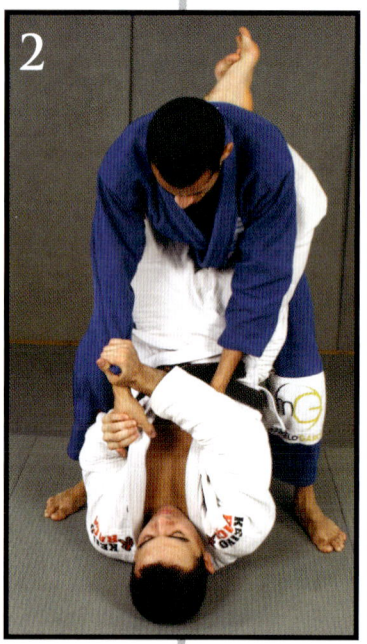

As Frank stands in an attempt to break open my guard, I keep my feet locked tightly together to keep him in my closed guard and grab his right sleeve with my right hand. To form my grip, I pinch the loose cloth at the edge of his sleeve with my thumb and index finger and then wrap my other fingers around the elevated fabric. Once accomplished, I wrap my left hand over the top of his right hand and prepare to rip his right grip off my left collar.

3

Keeping Frank in my closed guard, I use both hands to pry his right hand off my left collar.

4

The instant I break Frank's grip, I pull his right arm to the left side of his body using the grip I have on his right sleeve.

5

Still pulling Frank's right arm across his body, I underhook his right leg with my left arm and then use that control to pull my upper body close to his right leg. It is imperative to keep your guard closed until you manage to secure an underhook on your opponent's leg. If you don't, not only will your x-guard setup fail, but you will also run the risk of getting your guard passed.

ESTABLISHING THE X-GUARD 155

THE X-GUARD

6

Pulling Frank's right arm across his body using my right hand and controlling his right leg with my left hand, I unhook my feet and open my guard.

7

The moment I open my guard, I bring my knees to my chest and place my feet on Frank's hips. This positioning will allow me to push Frank away from me, offset his base, and create the space I need to secure my hooks.

8

Pushing Frank's body away from me using my legs, I create the space needed to secure my hooks. When executing this step, it is important to maintain tight control of your opponent's right leg using your left arm, as well as keep a tight grip on his right sleeve using your right hand.

9

Having created space, I maneuver my right leg to the back of Frank's left leg and slip my left foot to the inside of his left hip. Now that I have established both hooks, I can release my right grip on his sleeve and secure the x-guard position.

10

To secure the x-guard, I stretch out my legs, release my grip on Frank's right sleeve, and then wrap my right arm over the top of his right knee. Notice how I keep my hands locked tight around his leg to prevent him from pulling his leg out and escaping the position. I'm also keeping my legs tense to prevent him from escaping my hooks and advancing into a dominant position.

THE X-GUARD 👍 GI 👍 NO-GI

FULL GUARD TO X-GUARD (NO-GI / OPPONENT STANDING)

If you're training or competing no-gi, you can still transition into the x-guard from full guard when your opponent climbs to his feet. Just like in the previous technique, the first step is to gain control of his arm. However, because your opponent is not wearing a gi, you must latch on to his wrist rather than his sleeve. Once you have his arm, a common reaction is for him to rip his arm back, which will probably cause you to lose control of his arm. The instant this happens, you want to obtain control of his leg, which was your intention all along. If you had control of his right arm, you want to attack his right leg. If you had control of his left arm, you want to attack his left leg. After you've secured his leg, place both of your feet on your opponent's hips, push his weight back to create space, and then quickly establish the x-guard by securing both of your hooks.

1

Babs is locked in my closed guard.

2

In an attempt to break open my guard and pass to a dominant position, Babs climbs up to his feet.

158 THE X-GUARD

THE X-GUARD

ESTABLISHING THE X-GUARD

3

The instant Babs gets up to his feet, I grab the back of his right triceps with my left hand and grab the top of his right wrist with my right hand.

4

Using both hands, I maneuver Babs' right arm toward the left side of his body. It's important to note that this step is merely a ploy. The idea is to get your opponent to resist your control and rip his arm out of your grasp. As he does this, he creates the opening you need to secure control of his right leg.

5

To prevent me from controlling his arm, Babs pulls his right arm back and breaks my grips.

ESTABLISHING THE X-GUARD 159

THE X-GUARD

6

As soon as Babs pulls his arm away, I hook my left arm around the inside of his right leg and then use that control to rotate my body in a clockwise direction. At the same time, I place my right hand on the outside of his right knee. When executing these actions, it is important to keep your guard closed. If you open your guard before you have control of your opponent's leg, you'll not only fail at setting up the x-guard, but you also run the risk of getting your guard passed.

7

Still controlling Babs' right leg with both arms, I unlock my feet, draw my knees to my chest, and then place my left foot on his right hip and my right foot on his left hip. Once accomplished, I can then use my legs to push his body away from me, which will offset his base and create the space I need to secure both hooks.

8

I use my legs to push Babs' upper body away from me and create space. Notice how I maintain control of his right leg with both of my hands to prevent him from freeing his leg and escaping the position.

160 THE X-GUARD

9

To secure both hooks, I move my right leg to the back of Babs' left leg and slip my left foot to the front of his left hip.

10

To secure the x-guard, I pull Babs' right leg snug against my left shoulder. As I do this, I keep both of my legs tense to prevent him from escaping my hooks and advancing to a dominant position.

HALF GUARD TO X-GUARD (OPTION ONE)

I used to love working from the half guard at the beginning of my jiu-jitsu career, but as time passed, I discovered that certain opponents could give me a lot of trouble from the position, making it very difficult for me to sweep, submit, or even get back to full guard. I went on a hunt for a guard that would better my success rates, and eventually I found the x-guard. Now I only use the half guard as means to set up the x-guard. There are two techniques that I utilize to make this transition. Both moves are very similar—the only difference between them is how I establish my second hook. The technique I demonstrate here should be utilized when your opponent is stretched out in your half guard, giving you enough space to slip in your second hook without having to sit up. The technique I show next is for when your opponent maintains a sturdy base and hinders you from securing your second hook.

1. I've got Babs' right leg trapped between my legs in the half guard. Notice how I'm controlling the inside of his right biceps with my left arm.

2. Elevating Babs' right arm using my left hand, I move my right arm around his body and then shoot it underneath his right armpit.

3. Keeping my right arm pinned to the inside of Babs' right arm, I hook my left arm around the inside of his right leg just above his knee.

THE X-GUARD

THE X-GUARD

4

I open my guard and straighten both of my legs.

5

In order to make a smooth transition into the x-guard, I need to get my body out from underneath Babs' hips and move his right leg over my left shoulder. I start by rolling toward my right hip, pulling up on his right leg with my left underhook, and pushing on his right armpit with my right hand.

6

Rolling onto my right hip, I drive my right hand into Babs' right armpit and pull up on his right leg using my left underhook.

ESTABLISHING THE X-GUARD 163

THE X-GUARD

7

Having forced Babs' weight to my right side, I can now pull his right leg over my left shoulder using my left arm. Next, I curl my left leg over the top of his left leg. Notice how this traps his leg and prevents him from passing my guard.

8

To secure my bottom hook, I slide my right foot underneath Babs' left leg and then hook my foot around the back of his left calf.

9

Still controlling Babs' right leg using my left arm, I lift his left leg off the mat by curling my legs toward my chest. As I do this, I slide my right shin up his left leg.

THE X-GUARD

10

As Babs' base is lifted off the mat, I slip my left foot to the inside of his left thigh. It is important to mention that I use my right hand, along with my right leg, to prevent Babs from reestablishing his base.

11

To secure the x-guard, I hook my right hand over Babs' right leg and then clasp my left hand over the top of my right hand.

ESTABLISHING THE X-GUARD 165

THE X-GUARD | GI | NO-GI

HALF GUARD TO X-GUARD (OPTION TWO)

In the previous sequence I demonstrated how to transition from the half guard into the x-guard against a stretched-out opponent. Because he didn't have a sturdy base, you were able to lift his body using one leg, creating the space you needed to secure your second hook and form the x-guard. In this sequence, I show how to transition into the x-guard against an opponent who has a sturdy base. Using the last technique in this situation won't work because it'll be too hard to lift all of his weight using just one leg. In order to get your second hook, you need to use your free leg to rock yourself up into the sitting position. When done properly, this action creates the space you need to slip in your second hook and complete the transition.

1 I've established the half guard by trapping Babs' left leg between my legs. Notice how I'm controlling the inside of his right biceps with my left arm.

2 Elevating Babs' right arm using my left arm, I move my right hand around his body and shoot it underneath his right arm.

3 Keeping Babs' right arm elevated using my right arm, I slide my left arm to the inside of his right thigh.

THE X-GUARD

THE X-GUARD

4 — I hook my left arm around the inside of Babs' right leg.

5 — I open my guard by unhooking my feet and then elevate both of my legs off the mat.

6 — In one fluid motion, I roll toward my right side and pull Babs' right leg over my left shoulder using my left arm.

7 — To prevent Babs from passing my guard, I coil my left leg over his left leg and then plant my left foot on the mat.

ESTABLISHING THE X-GUARD

THE X-GUARD

8

I slide my right leg underneath Babs' left leg and then hook my right foot around the back of his left calf.

9

I rock forward and drive my right hand into Babs' right hip. This forces his body away from me and elevates his hips, creating the space I need to slide my right instep up his left leg. Notice how I wrap my right foot around the back of his left knee.

10

Continuing to push on Babs' right hip using my right hand, I straighten my left leg toward the ceiling.

THE X-GUARD

ESTABLISHING THE X-GUARD

11

To create the space I need to secure my top hook, I drive my left leg to the mat and use the momentum to sit upright.

12

To secure my top hook, I place my left leg over the top of my right leg and then slide my left foot to the inside of Babs' left thigh.

13

Maintaining tight control of Babs' right leg using my arms, I drop to my back and establish the x-guard position.

ESTABLISHING THE X-GUARD 169

OMOPLATA TO X-GUARD

The omoplata has become a major part of my game. Not only is it an excellent submission, but it's also an excellent gateway to the x-guard. Although I'm usually hunting for the finish when I slap on the omoplata, at times it can be a difficult technique to finish, especially if my opponent has tight defense or I don't have total control of his arm. If my opponent defends against the omoplata by posting his leg next to my head, and I feel as though I'm about to lose control of his arm, I'll immediately bail on the submission and transition into the x-guard by underhooking his posted leg, shoving my far leg to the inside of his hip, sitting up, and establishing my second hook. It's an excellent technique because so many jiu-jitsu practitioners will defend the omoplata in this fashion. Just when your opponent thinks he's escaped, you use his defense against him by transitioning to the x-guard. And once you get to the x-guard, you can sweep him to his back and work for the finish. Causing your opponent to tap from the omoplata is always best, but establishing the x-guard off a failed submission attempt is certainly nothing to complain about.

1

I've managed to trap Frank's right arm between my legs in the omoplata position.

2

In an attempt to escape the submission, Frank posts his right foot next to my head. The instant he does this, I hook my left arm tightly around the inside of his right leg and cup my right hand over his knee.

170 THE X-GUARD

3

Frank escapes the omoplata by pushing off his right foot and pulling his right arm out from between my legs. Immediately I hook my right foot around the back of his left knee. At the same time, I use my left leg to apply outward pressure to his back to force his upper body away from me, creating the space and leverage I need to sit up and establish my top hook.

4

Rocking my body forward, I sit up and lift Frank's right leg off the mat using my left arm. Next, I hook my left foot around the front of his left hip.

5

Using my hands to maintain tight control of Frank's right leg, I fall to my back and secure the x-guard position.

ESTABLISHING THE X-GUARD

THE X-GUARD   👍 GI   👍 NO-GI

MOUNT ESCAPE TO X-GUARD

It's obviously never a good idea to let your opponent obtain the mount position, but in certain situations it's hard to avoid. If you should find yourself stuck on your back with your opponent mounted on top of you, it's extremely beneficial to know how to escape into an advantageous position such as the x-guard. When you utilize this technique to reach such an end, there are two aspects that require special attention. The first and most important one is speed. As soon as you feel your opponent taking the mount, you should start working for your escape. If you allow your opponent to secure the position, not only will he have an assortment of attacks at his disposal, but he will also score points on the judges' scorecards. If you scramble and escape before he can secure the position, you rob him of his dominant positioning and any points he would have scored. The second aspect you need to pay special attention to is commitment. As you blast your hips off the mat, you need to drive your knee in-between your opponent's legs, secure your hook, gain control of his opposite leg, and then work for your second hook. If you execute the move without confidence and commitment, you won't get the desired results. It might take a little time to become proficient with the movements, but once you get the hang of quickly running through each of the steps, it becomes a priceless technique. I used it very effectively during one of my matches in the 2007 Abu Dhabi tournament.

1 Babs has managed to work into the mount, but before he can secure the position and begin his attack, I bring my heels to my butt and place both hands on his hips.

2 To elevate Babs' body, I push off the mat with both legs, explode my hips toward the ceiling, and drive his hips upward using my hands.

3 Extending my arms to keep Babs' body elevated, I slide my right knee to the inside of his left leg.

172   THE X-GUARD

THE X-GUARD

ESTABLISHING THE X-GUARD

4 I roll onto my right hip and push Babs' body to my right using both of my arms.

5 I slip my left hand underneath Babs' right leg and place my right hand on the outside of his right knee.

6 As I pull Babs' right leg up onto my left shoulder, I wrap my left arm around the outside of his leg and cup my left hand over his knee.

7 I draw my straightened left leg toward my head.

ESTABLISHING THE X-GUARD 173

THE X-GUARD

8

To create the space I need to secure my second hook, I drive my left leg to the mat and use the momentum to sit upright.

9

To secure my top hook, I place my left leg over the top of my right leg and then slip my left foot to the inside of Babs' left thigh.

10

Using both hands to maintain tight control of Babs' right leg, I drop to my back and secure the x-guard position.

FRONT HEAD CONTROL ESCAPE TO X-GUARD

There are many ways to end up on your elbows and knees, caught in the front headlock position. The most common way is when you shoot in for a takedown and your opponent sprawls and captures your head with his arms. It's to your advantage to escape this compromising position as quickly as possible, and utilizing this technique is an excellent way to accomplish that. Personally, I employ this move quite often in competition. The time clearest in my mind is when Mike Van Arsdale, a world-renowned wrestler, caught me in the front headlock position during our match in Abu Dhabi. Although he managed to avoid the x-guard by scrambling, the setup robbed his balance and forced him to let go of my head. If you plan on entering no-gi grappling competitions, which are filled with accomplished wrestlers who work well from the front headlock position, you definitely want this technique in your arsenal.

1 I'm down on all fours, stuck in the front headlock position.

2 To begin my escape to the x-guard, I post my left foot out on the mat.

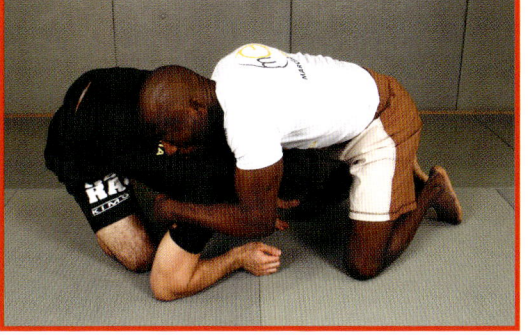

3 Posting on my left foot and right elbow, I slide my right leg underneath my left leg and then drop down to my right hip.

4

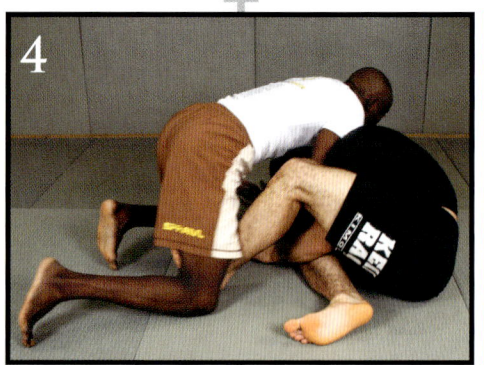

Falling to my right hip, I hook my left foot to the inside of Babs' right leg.

5

Rolling onto my right side, I drive my hands into Babs' hips and lift his right leg off the mat using my left butterfly hook.

6

Using my arms to keep Babs' hips elevated, I extend my left leg toward the ceiling to further lift his right leg off the mat.

THE X-GUARD

7

Still driving my hands into Babs' hips, I begin rotating my body in a clockwise direction, slip my right knee underneath his left leg, and place my right instep against his right thigh. At the same time, I straighten my left leg upward, causing Babs' right leg to slide toward the mat.

8

As Babs' right leg slides down my left leg, I hook my left arm underneath his right leg and wrap my right arm over his right hamstring.

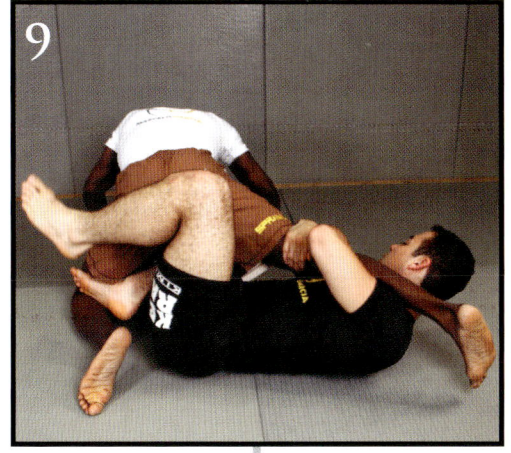

9

Using both hands, I move Babs' right leg over my left shoulder.

ESTABLISHING THE X-GUARD   177

THE X-GUARD

10

Now that I have control of Babs' right leg, I elevate my left leg toward the ceiling.

11

To create the space I need to secure my top hook, I drive my left leg toward the mat and use the momentum to sit upright.

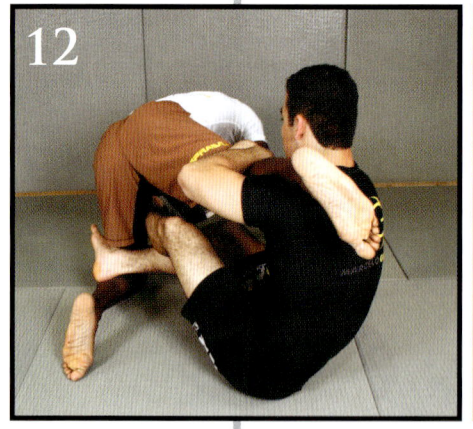

12

I secure my top hook by moving my left leg over the top of my right leg and then slipping my left foot to the font of Babs' left hip.

13

Using my arms to maintain control of Babs' right leg, I drop to my back and secure the x-guard position.

178 THE X-GUARD

THE X-GUARD

SWEEPS

Now that you understand how to establish the x-guard, it's time to delve into an array of techniques that allow you to sweep your opponent to his back. Each sweep is designed to combat your opponent's reaction to the position, which means you must acquire a technique for all his possible reactions. Whether he is standing, kneeling, grabbing, or running, you've got to have an attack for that particular scenario. The majority of those answers are laid out on the following pages, making it critical that you work on mastering the entire section. If you focus on just one sweep, you will only scratch the surface. To ensure success with the system, you must analyze all the techniques and discover how they can be sequenced together to deal with any reaction your opponent might have.

THE X-GUARD — GI / NO-GI

FAR SLEEVE CONTROL X-GUARD SWEEP (OPPONENT KNEELING)

Once you establish the x-guard position, deciding which sweep to utilize depends upon the positioning of your opponent. This particular sweep comes in handy when your opponent is on his knees, distributing his weight over your hooks and posting out on his far arm. Because his weight is back and his hands are on the mat, you can offset his base and sweep him over to his back by latching on to the sleeve of his far arm and pulling it toward your body with all of your might. Then it's just a matter of turning your hips toward the arm you're controlling and following him over to claim the top side control position. As with most x-guard sweeps, the most important part of the move is the underhook control that you establish on your opponent's leg. If you fail to secure proper control of his leg or you lose that control, not only will you fail to sweep your opponent to his back, but you will also run the risk of getting your guard passed. Next, I will show you two other variations of this sweep. The first one is the far wrist control x-guard sweep, which is a no-gi variation, and the other is designed to sweep your opponent when he is up on both feet. If you have trouble executing these sweeps, focus first on setting up and using the x-guard on one side or the other. Personally, I prefer to secure the x-guard by underhooking my opponent's right leg with my left arm and hooking my feet to the inside of his left leg. I almost always choose this side because I know I'll have no issues with maintaining proper x-guard positioning.

1

I've secured the x-guard position on Babs. Notice how he is leaning his weight back and posting on his left knee and hand.

2

I release my right grip on Babs' right knee and then prepare to reach my right hand toward his posted left hand.

3

Maintaining control of Babs' right leg using my left arm, I scoop my right arm around the back of his posted left hand and then grab the back of his sleeve. Notice how I have grabbed low on his sleeve rather than high up. This allows me to effortlessly pull his hand off the mat and steal his base.

4

To topple Babs' base, I pull his left arm toward my head using my right hand.

5

Still controlling Babs' right leg and left arm, I sweep him to the mat by rolling onto my right side and extending my hooks into his legs.

THE X-GUARD

6. As Babs is swept to his back, I work to establish the knee on belly position by removing my right hook from the back of his left leg, climbing up to my right knee, and maneuvering my left knee over his hips. At the same time, I release my right grip on his left sleeve and post on my right elbow. It is important to maintain control of your opponent's right leg using your left arm until you've completed the sweep and pinned your opponent's back to the mat by establishing the knee on belly position.

7. To secure the knee on belly position, I slide my left shin across Babs' hips. With his back now pinned to the mat, I establish head and arm control by releasing his right leg, wrapping my left arm underneath his right arm, sliding my right arm underneath his head, and clasping my hands together below his right shoulder.

8. To secure the side control position, I drive my left knee into Babs' left hip and drop my weight down on top of his torso.

182   THE X-GUARD

FAR WRIST CONTROL X-GUARD SWEEP

The far wrist control x-guard sweep is the no-gi variation of the previous technique—the only difference is how you grip your opponent's arm. Latching on to his sleeve obviously provides better control because you can rip his hand off the mat, but because you only need to control his arm for a split second to make the technique work, it can be pulled off utilizing wrist control. As a rule of thumb, techniques that rely upon establishing momentary grips translate well to no-gi, and those that depend upon maintaining grip control as you advance through a slow and methodical setup don't.

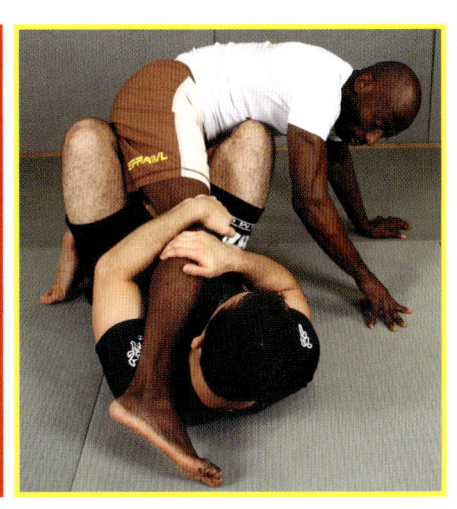

1. I've secured the x-guard position on Babs. Notice how he is leaning his weight back and posting on his left knee and hand.

2. I release my right grip on Babs' right knee.

3. Using my left arm to maintain control of Babs' right leg, I reach my right arm behind his posted left hand and grab the back of his wrist. It is important to notice my grip. My thumb is wrapped around the top of his wrist, and my fingers are wrapped around the back of his wrist. I have also established my grip low on his arm, which will allow me to effortlessly pull his hand off the mat and steal his base.

THE X-GUARD

4

To topple Babs' base, I pull his left arm toward my head using my right hand.

5

Maintaining control of Babs' left wrist and right leg, I extend both of my hooks into his right leg, roll onto my right side, and turn my whole body in a clockwise direction.

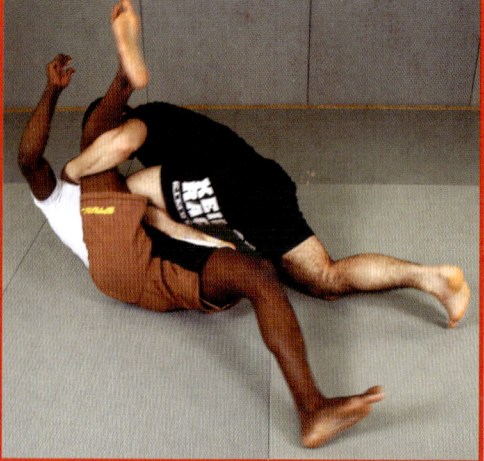

6

As Babs is swept to his back, I remove my right hook from behind his left knee, sprawl my right leg straight back, and then use my posted right knee to help push me into the top position. At the same time, I work to establish the knee on belly position by sliding my left shin across his hips.

7 — I secure the knee on belly position by sliding my left shin across Babs' hips, and then work my way into head and arm control by releasing his right leg, wrapping my left arm underneath his right arm, slipping my right arm underneath his head, and clasping my hands together below his right shoulder.

8 — To secure the side control position, I drive my left knee into Babs' left hip and bring my right knee up to his left shoulder.

FAR SLEEVE CONTROL X-GUARD SWEEP (OPPONENT STANDING)

A lot of jiu-jitsu practitioners have the misconception that you can only sweep your opponent using the x-guard when he is standing on both feet. Routinely I see competitors establish the x-guard on an opponent down on both knees, extend his hooks to force his opponent into the standing position, and then utilize an x-guard sweep. Although this can certainly work, it is completely unnecessary. The truth of the matter is it can actually be more difficult to sweep a standing opponent using the x-guard because he has a better base. Instead of simply rolling over your hips as you would against an opponent down on both knees, you have to rely more upon leverage and leg strength. In my opinion, this technique is best applied when you establish the x-guard on an opponent who is already standing. If he's down on his knees, I recommend using the technique I demonstrated at the beginning of this section.

1 I've secured the x-guard position on Babs.

2 I extend both of my hooks into Babs' left leg, forcing him to take an outward step with his left foot. Now that his base is stretched out, I remove my right hand from his knee and begin reaching for his left sleeve.

3 Keeping my legs extended to prevent Babs from reestablishing his base, I grip the top of his left sleeve with my right hand and begin pulling his arm toward my head.

4 I pull Babs' left arm to the right side of my head using my right hand.

5 Still pulling on Babs' left arm and controlling his right leg, I drive both of my hooks even harder into his left leg, forcing him to roll over onto his left shoulder. It is important to note that because your opponent is standing, you have to rely less on your hips and more on the power of your legs to topple his base and sweep him to his back.

THE X-GUARD

6

As Babs gets swept to his back, I remove my right hook from behind his left knee, sprawl my right leg back, and then use my posted right knee to help push me into the top position. At the same time, I establish the knee on belly position by placing my left knee across his hips. It's important to notice that I am still controlling Babs' right leg with my left arm. Not only does this control help me pull myself into the top position, but it also prevents an unnecessary scramble that could land me in Babs' guard.

7

To secure the knee on belly position, I slide my left shin across Babs' hips. Next, I establish head and arm control by releasing his right leg, sliding my left arm underneath his right arm, scooping my right arm underneath his head, and clasping my hands together beneath his right shoulder.

8

To secure side control, I place my left knee against Babs' left hip and bring my right knee up to his left shoulder.

188   THE X-GUARD

GI NO-GI   THE X-GUARD

NEAR SLEEVE CONTROL SWITCH SWEEP (OPPONENT KNEELING)

The x-guard was designed so that you'd have an answer for any action your opponent might make once he's trapped in the position. No matter how he behaves, you have a sweep for that particular situation. What usually happens is you attempt a sweep, your opponent counters the sweep, and you execute a second sweep based upon your opponent's counter. Sometimes this back-and-forth battle can go on for some time, but as long as you understand how to capitalize on his reactions, you'll eventually achieve your goal and put him on his back. A perfect example is the near sleeve control switch sweep, which is the technique I demonstrate below. As I reach for my opponent's near sleeve to establish a grip and gain control of his arm, he defends by pulling his arm back, which makes his opposite arm vulnerable to attack. Immediately I reach for his far arm, but he sees the attack coming and posts his arm outside of my grasp. However, in doing so he makes his near arm vulnerable again, and this time I am able to establish my grip, gain control of his sleeve, and then use that control to roll him over to his back. If you only know one x-guard sweep and encounter a situation like the one below, you'll get stuck. For this reason, it is very important to become proficient with the entire x-guard system.

1

I've secured the x-guard position on Babs. Notice how he is leaning his weight back and posting on his left knee and left hand.

2

Maintaining a solid grip on Babs' right leg using my left arm, I reach my right hand toward his right arm and try to grip the top of his sleeve.

SWEEPS 189

THE X-GUARD

3

Before I can secure a solid right grip on Babs' right sleeve, he pulls his arm back and breaks my hold.

4

The instant Babs pulls his right arm back, I reach my right hand toward his posted left arm. In this scenario, one of two things will happen. Either I'll secure control of his left arm, which will allow me to execute the far sleeve control x-guard sweep (p. 180), or he will prevent me from gaining control of his sleeve by moving his arm out of reach, which will allow me to attack his near arm and execute the near sleeve control switch sweep. No matter how my opponent reacts, I have an answer.

5

To prevent me from gaining control of his left arm by grabbing his left sleeve, Babs pulls his left hand out of reach.

THE X-GUARD

6

As soon as Babs pulls his left hand back, I pinch the cuff of his right sleeve between my index finger and thumb and then close the rest of my fingers around the elevated fabric.

7

Still controlling Babs' right leg with my left arm, I pull his right arm toward the mat using my right hand.

8

I drive Babs' right arm underneath his body and across his torso using my right hand.

SWEEPS 191

THE X-GUARD

9 I elevate Babs' left leg off the mat by extending both of my hooks into his left leg. It is important to notice that I'm still controlling his right leg and pushing his right arm underneath his body and across his torso.

10 I begin to elevate my legs and roll backward over my right shoulder.

11 To flip Babs over to his back, I continue to drive my hooks into his left leg and roll all the way over my right shoulder. As I do this, I keep both hooks intact and maintain control of his right leg using my left arm.

THE X-GUARD

12 Pushing myself backward over Babs' body, I remove my right hook from the back of his left leg and place my right knee underneath his left arm. To secure head and arm control, I wrap my right arm under his head, slip my left arm under his right arm, and clasp my hands together beneath his right shoulder.

13 To secure the side control position, I drop my left knee to the mat and place it against Babs' left hip.

THE X-GUARD — GI / NO-GI

NEAR WRIST CONTROL SWITCH SWEEP

This is the same sweep as the previous one, but instead of gaining control of my opponent's arm by latching on to his sleeve, I gain control of his arm by grabbing his wrist. It should be applied in the same situation as the last—your opponent's far arm is out of reach, so you immediately work to control his near wrist. Once you have that control, you push his arm toward his far hip and sweep him over to his back. It is important to mention that although this no-gi sweep works great when your opponent is down on both knees, it doesn't work so well when he is standing. The reason for this is because the setup takes longer, which means you must maintain control of your opponent's arm for more time—something that is difficult to manage without a sleeve to grip. However, this sweep works wonderfully against a standing opponent when grappling with a gi. To learn how this is done, visit the next technique in this section.

1 I've secured the x-guard position on Babs. Notice how he is leaning his weight back and posting on his left knee and hand.

2 Maintaining a solid grip on Babs' right leg using my left arm, I reach my right hand toward his right arm.

194   THE X-GUARD

3

I grab Babs' right wrist using my right hand. Notice how my fingers are wrapped around the top of his wrist and my thumb is wrapped around the bottom.

4

Still holding onto Babs' right leg using my left arm, I push his right wrist toward his left hip using my right hand.

5

To sweep Babs' to the mat using the switch sweep, I need to force him to roll forward over his right shoulder. To begin this process, I elevate his left leg by driving my hooks toward the ceiling. Notice how I continue to control his right leg and push his right arm underneath his body.

6

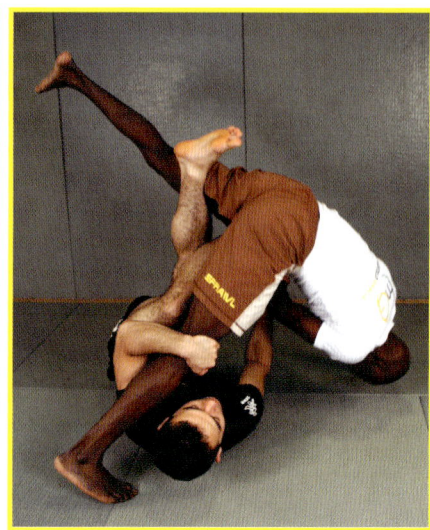

To force Babs to roll forward over his right shoulder, I continue to extend both of my hooks into his left leg and begin rolling backward over my right shoulder.

7

Rolling all the way over my right shoulder, I flip Babs over to his back. Notice how I keep both of my hooks intact to prevent him from scrambling.

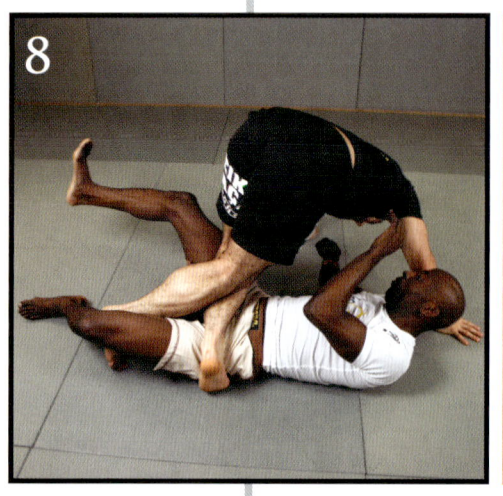

8

Continuing to drive both of my hooks into Babs' left leg, I move my left arm over his right leg and plant my hand on the mat. At the same time, I plant my right hand on the mat near the right side of his head. I then use both arms to push myself over the top of his body.

THE X-GUARD

9

As I center my body over Babs' torso, I remove my right hook from the back of his left leg and place my right knee up against his left arm.

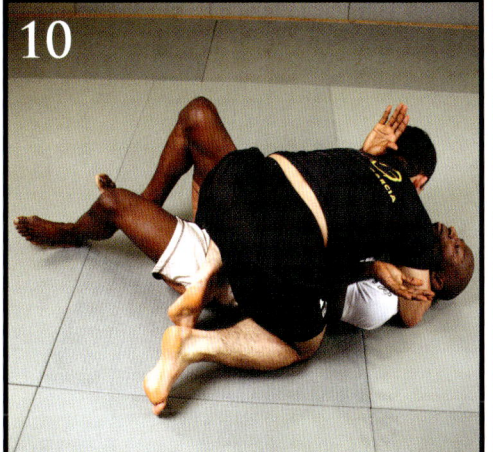

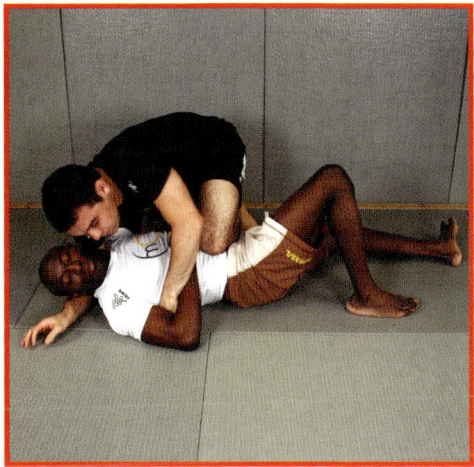

10

To begin establishing head and arm control, I wrap my right arm around Babs' head and wedge my left hand underneath his right armpit.

11

I secure head and arm control by slipping my left arm underneath Babs' right arm and clasping my hands together under his right shoulder. To secure side control, I slide my left knee down to Babs' left hip and place my right knee up against his left shoulder.

SWEEPS

THE X-GUARD 👍 GI 👎 NO-GI

NEAR SLEEVE CONTROL SWITCH SWEEP (OPPONENT STANDING)

This technique comes in handy in two scenarios: when you capture a standing opponent in the x-guard, and when you snare a kneeling opponent in the x-guard and he climbs to his feet in an attempt to avoid your sweeps. To acquire the leverage needed to complete the sweep, you must pull down on your opponent's arm and force him to bend over. This requires maintaining control of your opponent's arm for a healthy amount of time, which is difficult to manage when you don't have a sleeve to latch on to. For this reason, you should only attempt this move when competing in Brazilian Jiu-Jitsu or training exclusively with the gi.

I've secured the x-guard position on Babs. Notice how he is up on both feet and keeping his posture erect so that his weight is centered directly over my hips.

Maintaining control of Babs' right leg using my left arm, I grab his right sleeve with my right hand and then pull his arm toward the mat. Notice how this breaks his erect posture.

198 THE X-GUARD

THE X-GUARD

3

I push Babs' right arm toward his left ankle using my grip on his sleeve.

4

To execute the switch sweep, I need to elevate Babs' left leg and force him into a forward roll over his right shoulder. To begin this process, I extend both of my hooks upward and initiate a backward roll over my right shoulder. Notice how I maintain control of his right sleeve and right leg.

5

In one fluid motion, I roll backward over my right shoulder, extend both of my hooks into Babs' left leg, and drive my feet toward the mat. Notice how I've kept both hooks intact and maintained control of his right leg using my left arm. This prevents Babs from scrambling as I work to acquire the side control position.

SWEEPS

6 Continuing to drive both of my hooks into Babs' left leg, I move my left arm over his right leg and plant my hand on the mat. At the same time, I plant my right hand on the mat near the right side of his head. I then use both arms to push myself over the top of his body.

7 Using my arms to center my body over the top of Babs' torso, I establish the knee on belly position by keeping my left shin draped across his hips, removing my right hook from the back of his left leg, and then placing my right knee under his left arm. To begin securing head and arm control, I move my right arm to the left side of his head and slide my left arm underneath his right arm.

8 I secure head and arm control by clasping my hands together under Babs' right shoulder. To secure the side control position, I slide my left knee to the mat and drive it into his left hip.

NEAR SLEEVE AND ARMPIT CONTROL SWEEP

If you grab ahold of your opponent's near sleeve and he distributes the majority of his weight down by your legs, it can be difficult to get the sweep because he still has a strong base. A good way to eliminate his base is to pull his near arm across your body and grab his sleeve with your opposite hand (the one you have wrapped around his leg). However, this is easier said than done. If your opponent reacts by pulling his arm toward his body, which is quite common, it can become difficult to achieve your goal, especially if he's a good deal stronger than you. In such a situation, I'll remove one of my hooks, plant my foot in his armpit, and drive him over to his back. As I do this, I'll turn and obtain the top position. Sometimes you will fall right into side control, and other times you'll end up in your opponent's guard. Either way, you get the sweep.

I've secured the x-guard position on Babs. Notice how he is posting on his left knee and hand, pulling his weight away from my x-guard hooks. In order to pull of an effective sweep, I need to grab his near wrist and then use that control to sweep him over to his back.

Maintaining control of Babs' right leg using my left arm, I grab his right sleeve with my right hand and then pull his arm toward the mat. It is important to notice how I've gripped his sleeve. To achieve this grip, pinch the loose cloth at the edge of your opponent's sleeve with your thumb and index finger and then wrap your other fingers around the elevated fabric.

THE X-GUARD

3

In an attempt to escape the x-guard, Babs continues to pull his weight away from my hooks. I maintain control of the situation by elevating my shoulders off the mat and keeping tight control of his right leg and right sleeve.

4

Babs continues to pull away from my x-guard hooks. In order to sweep him over to his back, I need to use the energy of his escape against him. To begin, I plant my left foot in his right armpit.

5

Still pulling on Babs' right arm using my right hand, I drive the blade of my left foot into his right armpit and roll onto my right hip. By pushing and pulling on him at the same time, I've not only gained tremendous control over his right arm, but I'm also forcing him to roll over his right shoulder.

6

Continuing to pull Babs' right sleeve toward my body using my right hand, I roll over onto my right side and drive his right shoulder to the mat using my left leg. For the best results, it is important this step is done in one fluid motion.

202 THE X-GUARD

THE X-GUARD

7

I roll over onto my belly, post my left knee on the mat, and begin to corkscrew my body in a clockwise direction.

8

Still rotating my body in a clockwise direction, I release control of Babs' right leg, plant my left hand on the mat, and then use my left arm to keep my body upright.

9

I post my left foot on the mat, place my right instep over Babs' right thigh, and plant my right hand on the mat underneath his left armpit.

10

I grab Babs' right triceps using my left hand and pull his arm up. At the same time, I slide my right leg underneath my left leg. To secure side control, I settle my weight over the top of his torso.

SWEEPS

SLEEVE AND LEG CONTROL TAKEDOWN SWEEP

When you capture an opponent in the x-guard, his most common reaction will be to drop his weight down over your hooks and try to back out of your guard. To prevent this from happening, you want to maintain a tight trap on his leg using one hand and grab the sleeve of his near arm with your opposite hand. This allows you to control your opponent, but it will be difficult to sweep him from this position if he is still trying to back out of your guard because his weight won't be centered over your body. In such a situation, you have a couple of options. You can utilize the previous technique or you can pass his near sleeve over to the hand you're controlling his leg with. Once you're controlling both his leg and near arm with the same hand, your other hand gets freed up, which dramatically increases your sweeping options.

Deciding which option to choose should be based on how your opponent reacts to your positioning. If he continues to try and back out of your guard, you'll have the separation needed to execute the sleeve and leg control takedown sweep, which I demonstrate here. With this option, you use your free hand to help you sit upright and then climb to your feet, sweeping your opponent to his back in the process. You can also execute this technique no-gi, but because you don't have a sleeve to latch on to, you can't maintain control of your opponent's leg and near arm with the same hand, which makes the move slightly more difficult to manage. With both techniques, the one thing you really need to watch out for after sweeping your opponent to his back is getting caught in the triangle. You'll have one arm to the inside of his legs and one arm to the outside of his legs, giving him an opportunity to apply the submission. When I was competing in a national competition in 2006, I pulled this sweep off two or three times. Afterwards, a lot of people came up to me and asked, "Aren't you afraid of the triangle?" I wasn't worried about such an outcome because a submission was the last thing on my opponents' minds—they were all thinking about how not to get swept. Of course you have to be aware of your positioning. The instant you get the sweep, you want to focus on securing a solid base and begin passing your opponent's guard. If you are unable to immediately pass his guard, you'll want to bring your arms in tight to your body to avoid the triangle.

The second option you have for when you free up one hand is the sleeve and leg control reverse sweep, which I show after the next move. This technique should be employed when your opponent prevents you from climbing up to your feet by driving his weight back into you.

1

I've secured the x-guard position on Babs. Notice how he is leaning his weight back and posting on his left knee and left hand.

2

Maintaining a solid grip on Babs' right leg, I reach my right hand up and pinch the loose cloth at the edge of his right sleeve using the thumb and index finger of my right hand.

THE X-GUARD

3 Having pinched the loose cloth at the edge of Babs' right sleeve using the thumb and index finger of my right hand, I wrap my other fingers around the elevated fabric. As soon as I secure a solid grip, I pull his right arm toward my head.

4 I pass Babs' right arm over to my left hand.

5 I grip Babs' right sleeve with my left hand.

6 Controlling Babs' right arm and leg using my left arm and hand, I extend both of my hooks into his left leg, post my right hand on the mat, and sit up.

SWEEPS 205

THE X-GUARD

X-GUARD SWEEPS

7 Removing both of my x-guard hooks, I coil my legs toward my body and prepare to climb to my feet.

8 In one fluid motion, I push off the mat with my right hand and left foot, elevate my hips off the mat, slide my right leg underneath my left leg, and post my right foot on the mat underneath my hips.

9 Driving off my right foot, I step my left foot forward and place my right hand on Babs' left leg to prevent him from also coming up to his feet.

10 To secure the position, I release my grip on Babs' right sleeve and move my left arm to the inside of his left leg. This step is very important because having your arm wrapped around the outside of your opponent's leg can make you vulnerable to getting caught in a triangle choke. If you do not wish to reposition your left arm to the inside of your opponent's leg, you need to maintain good posture and be mindful of your positioning.

THE X-GUARD

TAKEDOWN SWEEP

This is the same sweep as the previous one, except here I demonstrate how to execute it when you're unable to grip your opponent's sleeve because he's not wearing a gi. I used this sweep in the 2005 Abu Dhabi tournament against Diego Sanchez, as well as in a number of other competitions. It's a highly effective technique because it's designed for opponents who attempt to back out of your guard, which is a very common reaction to the x-guard. In order to be successful with this technique, it is very important to explode up to your feet and use your opponent's backward momentum against him.

I've secured the x-guard on Babs. Notice how he is pulling his weight away from my x-guard hooks.

Controlling Babs' right leg using both of my arms, I extend my hooks into his left leg and sit up.

I remove both of my hooks, coil my heels toward my butt, and prepare to climb to my feet.

THE X-GUARD

X-GUARD SWEEPS

4 — Keeping my left foot posted on the mat, I reach my right arm across Babs' belt-line and hook my wrist around his left hip.

5 — In an attempt to escape, Babs hops up to his left foot.

6 — Still controlling Babs' right leg with my left arm, I come up to my right knee.

7 — I step my left foot forward, pull down on Babs' left leg with my right arm, and lift his right leg up with my left arm.

208 THE X-GUARD

THE X-GUARD

8 — Driving off my left foot, I stand up and lift Babs off the mat.

9 — I drop Babs to the mat.

10 — I drop my left knee to the mat next to Babs' left hip, move my right arm over his left arm, and then slide my right hand underneath his neck.

11 — To secure side control, I drop my right knee to the mat next to Babs' left shoulder, wrap my right arm around the back of his neck, and drop my chest on the top of his torso.

SWEEPS 209

SLEEVE AND LEG CONTROL REVERSE SWEEP (OPPONENT KNEELING)

Just like the sleeve and leg control takedown sweep, this technique comes into play when your opponent attempts to back out of your x-guard. It is set up the same in that you want to gain control of both your opponent's leg and near arm using one hand, freeing up your opposite arm in the process. If your opponent continues to try and back out of your guard when you establish this positioning, the takedown sweep is an excellent option. However, a lot of times your opponent will prevent you from climbing to your feet by driving his weight back into you. In such a situation, you'll want to shift gears and pull off the sleeve and leg control reverse sweep, which I demonstrate here. To accomplish this, reach your free hand up and latch on to your opponent's lapel. If his lapel is too far away, grab the shoulder of his gi. Once you have your grips, you'll want to reassess the situation. If your opponent continues to drive into you, remove your x-guard hooks, place your feet on his hips, lift his body into the air, and sweep him over to his back as I demonstrate below. If he decides to pull away from you again and try to escape your x-guard, transition back to the takedown sweep. As long as you have both of these sweeps perfected and can transition back and forth between them, you'll catch your opponent between a rock and a hard place.

1) I've secured the x-guard position on Babs. Notice how he is leaning his weight back and posting on his left knee and left hand.

2) Maintaining control of Babs' right leg using my left arm, I remove my right hand from his right leg and reach toward his right arm.

3) I pinch the edge of Babs' right sleeve using my right thumb and index finger and then wrap my other fingers around the elevated fabric. The instant I have a solid grip, I pull his right arm toward my head.

THE X-GUARD

X-GUARD SWEEPS

4

To free up my right hand, I move Babs' right arm toward my left arm and then use my left hand to secure the same type of grip on his right sleeve as I did in the previous step.

5

As soon as I establish my left grip on Babs' right sleeve, I grab his gi just above his shoulder with my right hand.

6

Maintaining control of Babs' right leg and arm using my left arm and hand, I extend both of my hooks into his left leg and sit up.

SWEEPS   211

THE X-GUARD

7 Sitting all the way up, I uncross my feet, place my right foot on the inside of Babs' left hip, and place my left foot on the inside of his left thigh.

8 In one fluid motion, I roll to my back, push on Babs' left thigh with my left foot, push on his left hip with my right foot, and pull his lapel toward me using my right hand.

9 Continuing to roll to my back, I push on Babs' left thigh with my with left foot, push on his left hip with my right foot, and pull his lapel toward me using my right hand.

212   THE X-GUARD

10

As I execute a backward roll over my right shoulder, I sweep Babs to his back. Notice how I keep my left foot pinned to his left leg as I flip him over to the mat.

11

Using the momentum of my backward roll, I push myself into side control on Babs' left side. The instant I land in the position, I bring my left knee up to his left hip, place my right knee against his left shoulder, and then work for head and arm control by wrapping my right arm around the back of his head and wedging my left hand underneath his right arm.

12

To secure the position, I clasp my hands together underneath Babs' right shoulder.

SLEEVE AND LEG CONTROL REVERSE SWEEP (OPPONENT STANDING)

The sleeve and leg control reverse sweep can also be done from the standing position, but it is considerably more risky. Just as in the previous technique, you need to release your x-guard hooks and place both feet on your opponent's hips in order to get the sweep, but because your opponent is now standing, he'll have a brief window of opportunity to escape. The key to success with this technique is speed and timing. Although it's not the safest technique available in the x-guard system, it's a beautiful sweep and highly effective when done correctly. I know this to be true because I pulled it off against a high-level jiu-jitsu player in the Mundials.

1 I've secured the x-guard position on Babs. Notice how he is up on both feet, keeping his posture straight so that his weight is centered directly over my hips.

2 In order to get offensive, I need to stretch out Babs' legs and strip his base. I accomplish this by extending both of my hooks into his left leg, forcing him to take an outward step with his left foot.

3 Still controlling Babs' right leg using my left hand, I grip the top of his left sleeve with my right hand.

214 THE X-GUARD

THE X-GUARD

4 To gain control of Babs' right arm, I pinch the edge of his left sleeve with my right thumb and index finger and then wrap my other fingers around the elevated fabric. As soon as I secure a solid grip, I pull his right arm toward my head.

5 To free up my right arm, I pass Babs' right arm over to my left hand.

6 I grip Babs' right sleeve with my left hand.

7 I grab the inside of Babs' right collar with my right hand.

SWEEPS 215

THE X-GUARD

8

Still controlling Babs' right leg and arm using my left arm and hand, I pull down on his lapel with my right hand.

9

I place my right foot on Babs' left hip, and I place my left foot on the inside of his left thigh.

10

In one fluid motion, I push on Babs' left thigh with my left foot, push on his left hip with my right foot, and pull his lapel toward me using my right hand. It is important to notice that during this I've used my left arm to maintain control of his right leg and arm.

216 THE X-GUARD

11

I roll backward over my right shoulder, sweeping Babs to his back. It is important to keep your left foot pinned to your opponent's left leg as you flip him over to the mat.

12

Using the momentum of my backward roll, I push myself into side control on Babs' left side. As soon as I land, I bring my left knee up to his left hip, my right knee up to his left shoulder, and begin working for head and arm control by wrapping my right arm around the back of his head and wedging my left hand underneath his right arm.

13

To secure the position, I clasp my hands together underneath Babs' right shoulder.

SLEEVE AND LEG CONTROL X-GUARD SCISSOR SWEEP

Sometimes when you secure the x-guard on an opponent, he will stand erect and form a solid base instead of trying to bail out the back door. Although this hinders you from climbing to your feet and executing the takedown sweep, it sets you up to utilize the sleeve and leg control x-guard scissor sweep. You accomplish this by gaining control of his near sleeve with your free hand, passing his arm off to the hand you're controlling his leg with, and then sweeping him to the mat by lifting with your bottom hook and pushing with your top hook. In order to be successful, you need to employ the full strength of your legs as you lift and push to stretch your opponent out, which makes him lighter and robs him of balance. Once he goes down, it is important to immediately remove your hooks and sit up to ensure that you secure the top position. If you can't execute this sweep because your legs are too short, your opponent is too tall, or your opponent counters by stepping his leg closer to your body, you'll want to use the next technique in this section.

1
I've secured the x-guard position on Babs. Notice how he is up on both feet and keeping his back straight so that his weight is centered directly over my hips.

2
Maintaining a solid grip on Babs' right leg using my left arm, I reach my right hand upward and pinch the loose cloth at the edge of his right sleeve with my thumb and index finger.

3
Having pinched Babs' right sleeve using my right thumb and index finger, I wrap my other fingers around the elevated fabric. As soon as I form a solid grip, I pull his right arm down and begin passing it to my left hand.

THE X-GUARD

4 To free up my right hand, I grab Babs' right sleeve with my left hand. I then place my right hand on his right knee and begin to push.

5 Babs keeps his posture straight and his weight centered. To sweep him over to his back, I drive my left hook up into his left hip and extend my right leg upward into his left hamstring. It's important to notice that I'm still controlling his right leg and arm with my left hand, as well as pushing his right knee outward using my right hand.

6 I sweep Babs to his back by extending both of my hooks into his left leg. Notice how I'm still controlling his right leg and arm with my left arm. This prevents him from blocking the sweep by posting his right hand on the mat. Also notice how I'm still pushing on his right knee with my right hand to prevent him from scrambling to his feet and escaping.

SWEEPS

THE X-GUARD

7

Still controlling Babs' right arm and leg with my left arm, as well as maintaining my grip on his right knee with my right hand, I remove my x-guard hooks and coil both of my heels toward my buttocks.

8

Turning into Babs' guard, I release my grip on his right arm, plant my right foot on the mat, and climb up to my left knee. At the same time, I place my right hand behind his left knee to avoid getting caught in a triangle choke.

9

Continuing to turn into Babs' guard, I step my right foot forward and place my hands on the top of his legs. From here I can work to pass his open guard.

SLEEVE AND LEG CONTROL X-GUARD PUSH SWEEP

When you attempt the previous sweep, sometimes it will be difficult to stretch your opponent out far enough to strip his base and topple him to the mat. Oftentimes, you'll be able to force him to take an outward step, but you simply can't finish him with the scissor sweep. This can happen for several reasons, such as your legs are too short, your opponent is too strong, he has exceptional balance, or he manages to counter the sweep by stepping his leg closer to your body. If you are faced with any one of these scenarios, a good option is to transition to this sweep. To begin, you want to secure control of your opponent's near sleeve with the same arm that is controlling his leg. Once you've established that control, you can use your free hand to latch on to his near leg. From there, all you have to do is drive him down to his back by pushing into him using your x-guard hooks.

1. I've secured the x-guard position on Babs. Notice how he is up on both feet and keeping his back straight so that his weight is centered directly over my hips.

2. Maintaining a solid grip on Babs' right leg using my left arm, I remove my right hand from his knee and pinch the loose cloth at the edge of his right sleeve between my right thumb and index finger.

3. Having pinched the edge of Babs' right sleeve between my index finger and thumb, I close the rest of my fingers around the elevated fabric. As soon as I have a solid grip, I pull his right arm toward my torso.

THE X-GUARD

4 — I pass Babs' right sleeve to my left hand and form the exact same grip as I did in the previous step. Once I have a firm grip, I place my right hand on his right knee to prevent him from stepping his right leg over my head and escaping the position.

5 — I attempt to sweep Babs to the mat utilizing the 'sleeve and leg control x-guard scissor sweep' by extending both of my hooks into his left leg, but Babs counters by stepping his left foot out.

6 — Due to Babs' defensive actions, his base is too strong for the scissor sweep to be effective. Changing tactics, I relax both of my hooks. No longer stretched out, Babs steps his left leg closer to my body in an attempt to improve his base.

THE X-GUARD

7

The instant Babs steps his left foot closer to my body, I remove my right hand from his knee and grab his left instep.

8

Still controlling Babs' right leg and arm with my left hand, I pull on his left ankle with my right hand and drive both of my hooks into his left leg. Notice how this causes him to fall backward.

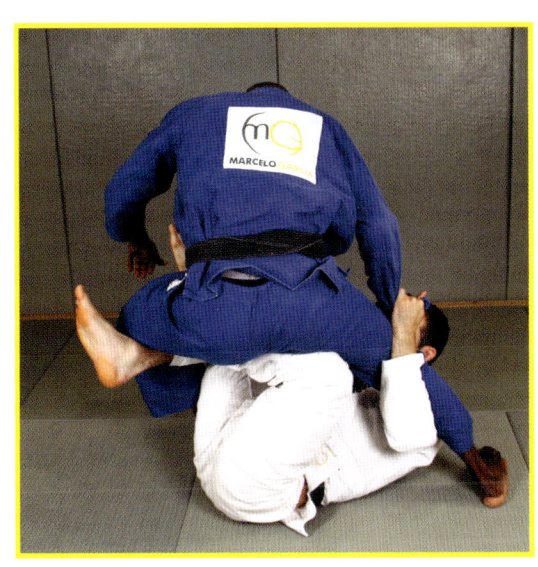

9

I continue to pull on Babs' left ankle with my right hand and drive both of my legs into his left leg.

SWEEPS 223

THE X-GUARD

10

As Babs is forced to his back, I sit up.

11

I remove both of my hooks and coil my heels toward my buttocks.

12

I stand up. Notice how I'm still controlling both of Babs' legs to prevent him from scrambling up to his feet as I work to establish top control.

13

I step my left leg back and move both hands to the inside of Babs' legs to prevent myself from getting caught in a triangle choke. From here I can work to pass his open guard.

GI NO-GI   THE X-GUARD

X-GUARD PUSH SWEEP

In the previous sequence I demonstrated how to secure control of your opponent's near sleeve, snare his rear leg with your free hand, and then collapse him to his back by driving your hooks into his body. In this sequence, I demonstrate the no-gi version of the same technique. When done correctly, it's highly effective. I use it all the time in competition. As a mater of a fact, I managed to pull it off on the legendary Renzo Gracie in the 2003 Abu Dhabi Submission Wrestling World Championships. You've got to figure that if it works on a jiu-jitsu fighter as accomplished and technical as Renzo, it will work on just about anybody. The main thing you need to focus on when utilizing this technique is speed and timing. As soon as you feel your opponent step his rear leg toward your body, you want to snatch up his foot with your free hand, pull his leg toward your body, drive into him using your legs, and then sit up to secure top control.

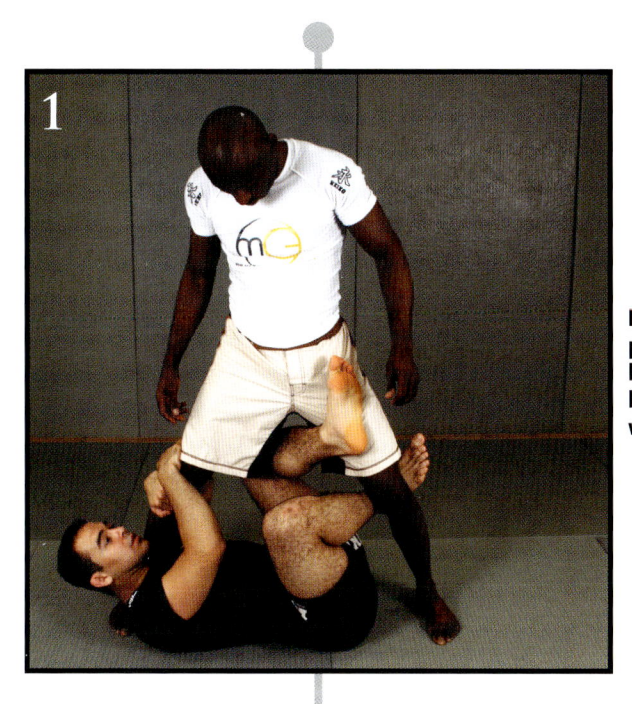

1 I've secured the x-guard position on Babs. Notice how he is standing with his back straight, centering his weight over my hips.

2 I attempt to sweep Babs to the mat by extending both of my hooks into his left leg, but he counters by taking a long, outward step with his left leg.

SWEEPS 225

THE X-GUARD

3

Having stepped his left leg back, Babs' base is too strong from his current position to sweep him to the mat. Changing my tactics, I relax my legs so that he can step his left leg closer to my body. The instant he does this, I remove my right hand from his right knee and grab the outside of his left instep.

4

Still controlling Babs' right leg with my left arm, I pull his left ankle toward my head using my right hand.

5

To sweep Babs to the mat, I extend both of my hooks into his left leg while continuing to pull his left ankle toward my head.

226 THE X-GUARD

THE X-GUARD

6

As Babs falls to his back, I sit up.

7

I remove both of my x-guard hooks and post my feet on the mat.

8

Controlling both of Babs' legs to prevent him from scrambling, I climb to my feet. Once up, I move both of my hands to the inside of his legs to prevent from getting caught in a triangle choke. From here I can work to pass his open guard.

SWEEPS

THE X-GUARD 👍 GI 👎 NO-GI

SLEEVE AND LEG CONTROL PUSH SWEEP VARIATION

As you're probably aware by now, the x-guard sweeps laid out in this book are based upon your opponent's reaction to the position. No matter how he behaves when you snare him in the x-guard, you should have a sweep tailor made for that particular scenario. However, it is important to keep in mind that the majority of the time your initial sweep attempts will fail, either because your opponent realizes your intentions or he counters your movement instinctively. In order to become an x-guard master, it is essential that you learn how to string sweeps together. It's not enough to understand what sweep to pull out of your arsenal based upon your opponent's first reaction to the position—you must also know what sweep to utilize based upon his counter to your original sweep. To give you an example, I'll plug the technique I demonstrate on this page into a hypothetical sweeping combination: Having snared your opponent in the x-guard, you begin your attack with the x-guard scissor sweep by stretching his legs apart. Realizing he is in danger of being swept, your opponent counters by drawing his rear leg toward your body. Although his action hinders you from completing your first sweep, it opens the door for you to execute the x-guard foot sweep. As you work through the steps of the move, your opponent again counters by dropping down to one knee. This distributes a large portion of his weight over your body, which prevents you from completing the x-guard push sweep. In the current situation using the strength of your legs to sit up and sweep your opponent to his back is not an option because too much of his weight is centered over your body, so instead you transition to the sleeve and leg control x-guard push sweep variation, which is the technique I demonstrate below. You accomplish this by maintaining control of your opponent's foot, removing your top hook, and then using your free leg to generate enough momentum to sit up and sweep your opponent to his back. If you do not understand how to use your opponent's counters against him, a scenario such as the one I just described would not be possible.

1

I've secured the x-guard position on Babs. Notice how he is standing with his back straight, centering his weight over my hips.

2

Maintaining a solid grip on Babs' right leg using my left arm, I pinch the edge of his right sleeve between my right thumb and index finger and then coil my other fingers around the elevated fabric.

THE X-GUARD

3

The instant I have a solid grip on Babs' right sleeve, I pull his arm toward my body and then pass his sleeve over to my left hand.

4

I grab Babs' right sleeve with my left hand. With my right hand now free, I place my palm on his right knee and begin to apply outward pressure.

5

I extend both of my hooks into Babs' left leg, causing him to take an outward step.

SWEEPS 229

THE X-GUARD

6 Having forced Babs to take an outward step, I would normally attempt to execute the 'sleeve and leg control scissor sweep,' but in this particular case, he has an exceptionally strong base. Changing my tactics, I relax my legs and allow him to step his left foot closer to my body.

7 The instant Babs steps his left leg closer to my body, I remove my right hand from his knee and grab the outside of his left instep. From here I can work to sweep him to the mat utilizing the 'sleeve and leg control x-guard push sweep.'

8 Keen to my intentions, Babs counters the 'sleeve and leg control x-guard push sweep' by dropping his right knee to the mat.

THE X-GUARD

9

Maintaining control of Babs' right arm and left foot, I roll backward and extend my right leg into his left leg.

10

As Babs' left leg is forced upward, I pull my left leg out from underneath his left leg. Next, I straighten my left leg and draw it back toward my head.

11

I kick my straightened left leg toward the mat and then use the momentum to sit upright.

SWEEPS 231

THE X-GUARD

13

Still controlling Babs' right leg and arm using my left arm, pulling up on his left foot with my right hand, and extending my right leg into his left leg, I sit up and drive him over to his back.

14

I bring both feet in close to my body and stand up. Notice how I maintain control of Babs' legs to prevent him from scrambling.

15

Stepping my left leg back, I move both hands to the inside of Babs' legs to prevent myself from getting caught in a triangle choke. From here I can work to pass his open guard.

X-GUARD PUSH SWEEP VARIATION

As you learned in the previous introduction, the x-guard push sweep is an excellent technique to utilize when your opponent counters the regular x-guard push sweep by dropping his knee down to the mat and centering his weight over your body. However, when grappling without a gi the previous x-guard push sweep variation isn't an option because it requires you to latch on to your opponent's uniform. In the sequence below, I show you how to modify your grips when you're training or competing without a gi.

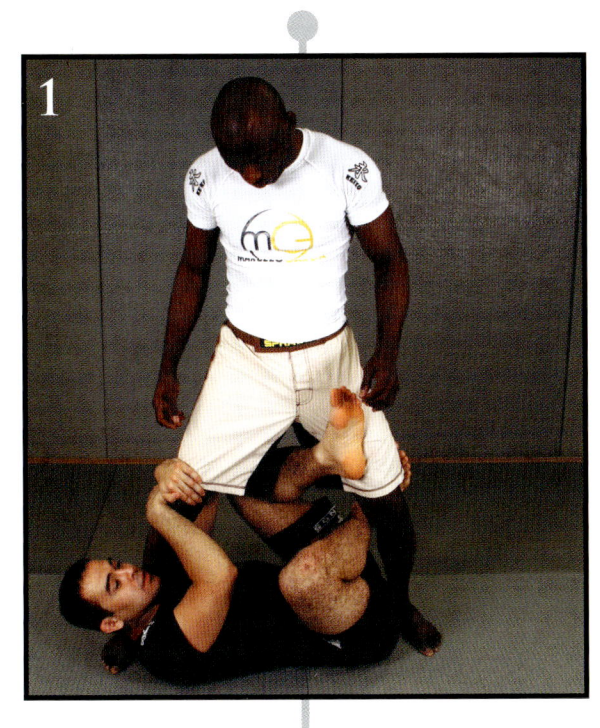

1

I've secured the x-guard position on Babs.

2

I drive both of my hooks into Babs' left leg, causing him to take an outward step. Unfortunately, he maintains his balance by keeping his posture straight and his weight centered, making it difficult for me to execute a sweep.

THE X-GUARD

3

Although I have Babs stretched out, it will be difficult for me to sweep him from his current positioning due to his strong base. To set him up for a different sweep, I relax my legs and allow him to step his left leg closer to my body.

4

The instant Babs steps his left leg closer to my body, I remove my right hand from his right knee and grab the outside of his left instep. From here I can work to sweep him to the mat utilizing the x-guard push sweep.

5

Realizing my intentions, Babs counters the push sweep by dropping his right knee to the mat.

THE X-GUARD

6

The moment Babs' right knee hits the mat, I roll back and elevate his left leg off the mat by extending my right leg toward the ceiling. Notice how I'm still maintaining control of his left ankle with my right hand.

7

I pull my left leg out from underneath Babs' left leg and cock it back toward my head.

8

I kick my straightened left leg toward the mat, pull on Babs' left ankle with my right hand, and drive my right leg into his left leg.

SWEEPS 235

THE X-GUARD

9

As my actions cause Babs to fall to his back, I sit up, coil my heels toward my buttocks, and plant both feet on the mat. Notice how I'm still controlling both of his legs.

10

As I stand up, I make sure to control Babs' legs to prevent him from scrambling.

11

Widening my base by stepping my left leg out to the side, I move both of my hands to the inside of Babs' legs to prevent myself from getting caught in a triangle choke. From here I can work to pass his open guard.

SLEEVE AND LEG CONTROL PULL BACK SWEEP

Sometimes when I capture a taller opponent in the x-guard, gain control of his near sleeve, and attempt to stretch him out, he is able to maintain his base. If I'm controlling his leg with my left arm, I'll immediately pass his leg over my head and to the outside of my right arm. As you will shortly see, your opponent's height will not hinder you from sweeping him from this new position. To learn how to modify this move when grappling without a gi, take a look at the next sequence in this section.

1 I've secured the x-guard position on Babs. Notice how he is standing erect, centering his weight over my hips.

2 Maintaining a solid grip on Babs' right leg using my left arm, I pinch the loose cloth at the edge of his right sleeve between my right index finger and thumb and then clasp my other fingers around the elevated fabric. Once I have a solid grip, I pull his right arm toward my torso.

THE X-GUARD

3

I push up on Babs' right leg with my left hand and begin moving his right leg over my head.

4

I guide Babs' leg so that he plants his foot to the outside of my right arm. If your opponent steps to the inside of your right arm, you'll have to quickly release your grip on his right sleeve and work to sweep him using the pull back sweep, which is the next technique shown in this section.

5

Pulling on Babs' right arm with my right hand, I remove my left hand from the back of his right leg and cock my arm behind my head.

THE X-GUARD

6

I thrust my left arm forward and use the momentum to sit upright. As I come up, I wedge my left hand underneath Babs' right arm and cup my wrist around his biceps.

7

Still controlling Babs' right sleeve with my right hand, I pull his right arm toward my head using my left hand. At the same time, I extend my hooks upward and roll to my back.

8

I continue to roll to my back and extend my hooks upward into Babs' left leg.

SWEEPS

THE X-GUARD

9

As I roll onto my shoulders, Babs gets flipped over onto his back. If I were to continue with my backward roll and keep my hooks intact, I would end up in his guard. To avoid this outcome, I release my x-guard hooks.

10

I roll over my left shoulder and get up to my knees. Notice how I'm still using my hands to control Babs' right leg.

11

Maintaining my right grip on Babs' right sleeve, I center my torso over his body and wrap my left arm under his neck to establish top control.

THE X-GUARD

X-GUARD PULL BACK SWEEP

If you're grappling with a gi and are unable to execute an x-guard sweep on a standing opponent due to his height, you want to utilize the previous move. In the sequence below, I demonstrate how to modify your grips to execute the no-gi version of the same technique.

1

I've secured the x-guard position on Babs. Notice how he is standing erect so that his weight is centered over my hips.

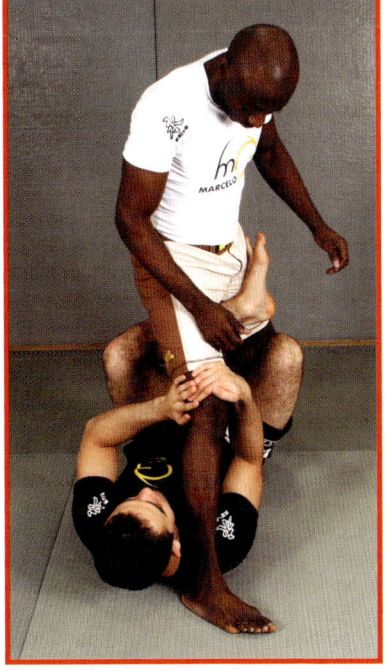

2

Babs steps his right leg over my head and plants his foot between my neck and right shoulder.

SWEEPS 241

THE X-GUARD

3

To sweep Babs to the mat, I force his right leg toward my left side by pulling on it with my left hand and pushing on it with my right hand. At the same time, I lift his left leg off the mat using my hooks.

4

Continuing to lift Babs' left leg and force his right leg to my left side, he begins to lose balance.

5

As Babs lands on the mat, I roll onto my left side and straighten my left leg.

242   THE X-GUARD

THE X-GUARD

Keeping my right arm hooked around Babs' right leg, I plant my right foot on the mat and begin to work up to my knees.

I pull my left leg out from underneath my right leg and then post my left knee next to Babs' right arm.

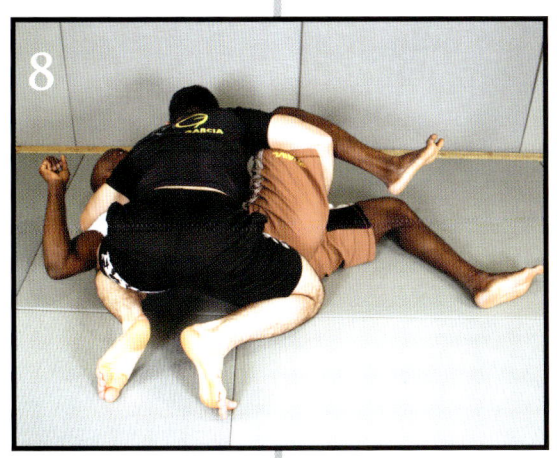

To secure top control, I place my right knee against Babs' hips, wrap my left arm underneath his head, and settle my weight down on his torso. Notice how I keep my left arm hooked around his right leg as I secure the top position.

SWEEPS 243

THE X-GUARD

SUBMISSIONS

Although the x-guard is designed for sweeps, incorporating submissions is a vital part of the system. Not only can they allow you to finish the fight on a moment's notice, but they also give your opponent something to constantly worry about, which spreads his focus thin. Anytime you add another aspect to your game, you become a more dangerous competitor.

OMOPLATA

From time to time when I'm training or competing in Brazilian Jiu-Jitsu, I'll transition from the x-guard into the omoplata submission. It's not one of those moves that you'll be able to pull out of your hat in every competition, but it's a nice transition to have in your arsenal nonetheless. The best time to employ this move is when your opponent is down on his knees trying to escape from your x-guard. In order to be successful, you need to latch on to his near sleeve to trap his arm. If he manages to free his arm before you pull off the submission, you'll be in a bad spot, which is the reason this technique should only be employed when your opponent is wearing a gi to latch on to. Once you've got his arm trapped, swing your leg over into the omoplata position, keep your legs as heavy as possible to prevent him from standing up, and then sit up and finish the submission.

1 I've secured the x-guard position on Babs. Notice how he is posting on his left knee and hand and leaning his weight back.

2 Maintaining a solid grip on Babs' right leg using my left arm, I pinch the edge of his right sleeve between my right index finger and thumb and then close my other fingers around the elevated fabric. Once I have a solid grip, I pull his right arm toward my head.

THE X-GUARD

3 Maintaining my right x-guard hook, I place my left foot into Babs' right armpit and sit up.

4 Still controlling Babs' right leg and right sleeve, I rotate my body in a clockwise direction and drop to my back. As I do this, I move my right leg out from underneath Babs' body and hook my left leg around the back of his right shoulder.

5 I hook my right foot over the top of my left foot, pinch my knees together, and then straighten out my legs. This breaks Babs' posture and forces his head to the mat. Notice how I've maintained control of his right leg and right sleeve. The former prevents him from freeing his leg and escaping the position, and the latter keeps him from freeing his arm and escaping the omoplata submission.

SUBMISSIONS 247

6 I curl my right leg behind me, coil my left leg around Babs' right arm, release my left grip on his right leg, and sit up. Once I'm up, I wrap my left arm around his back, reach my left hand underneath his left arm, and then grip his left collar with my left hand for control.

7 I jam my right hand underneath Babs' right shoulder and pull my upper body toward his head. To complete the submission, I then drive his right shoulder down using my left leg while pulling his right forearm upward by elevating my hips.

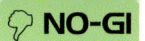

TRIANGLE

I firmly believe that all jiu-jitsu practitioners should focus on perfecting positions that will work for them the majority of the time. Early in my jiu-jitsu career, I was obsessed with the triangle. No matter what position I was in or whom I was grappling with, I'd go for it time and again. I was determined to become a triangle master. It wasn't until I got more advanced that I realized I hadn't spent my time too wisely. Although the triangle worked great against opponents in my division, it didn't work well against opponents who were larger than me due to my short legs. With this realization, I abandoned my quest to have the best triangle in the business and focused instead on developing a mean x-guard, which works against all opponents, not just guys my size. I haven't forgotten what I need to do to capture my opponent in a triangle, but due to my refocused efforts, I no longer have the conditioning the position requires to be effective. I might have lost something by following the philosophy "do what works the majority of the time," but I became a lot more dangerous in the long run.

1. I've secured the x-guard on Babs. Notice how he is pulling away from my hooks.

2. Maintaining a solid grip on Babs' right leg using my left arm, I pinch the edge of his right sleeve between my right index finger and thumb.

THE X-GUARD

3

Having pinched the edge of Babs' right sleeve between my right index finger and thumb, I close my other fingers around the elevated fabric.

4

Babs continues to pull away from my x-guard hooks in an attempt to escape the position. Instead of fighting him, I use his resistance to help me sit up. Notice how I'm still controlling his right leg and right sleeve.

5

As soon as I sit up, I release my x-guard hooks by coiling my legs inward.

250 THE X-GUARD

6

Pulling on Babs' right arm using my right hand, I roll to my back and straighten my legs. Notice that my left leg is positioned between his right leg and arm, and my right leg is on the left side of his neck.

7

I coil my left leg around Babs' lower back. At the same time, I place my left hand on his right elbow and then use that control, along with my right grip on his sleeve, to force his right arm across my hips. Once accomplished, I wrap my right leg around the left side of his head.

8

To lock in the triangle, I wrap my left leg over my right foot and squeeze my knees together.

INVERTED ARMBAR (GI)

In the first section of this book I demonstrated several ways to sweep a kneeling opponent when he attempts to escape your x-guard by pulling away from you or standing up. In this scenario, your opponent does neither. Instead, he attempts to maintain his balance and base by remaining on his knees and latching on to your collar. Although his actions make it difficult for you to stretch out his base and sweep him over to his back, it gives you an opening to execute the inverted armbar. To apply the submission, pull his hand up over your shoulder the instant he grabs your collar. For example, if he grabs your collar with his right hand, you want to pull his hand over your left shoulder using your right hand. Next, release the trap you have on his leg to free up an arm, and then throw that arm over his captured arm. Once accomplished, securing the submission is simply a matter of applying downward pressure. You'll get more leverage if you're able to sit up, but it isn't always possible. Also, it is important not to slide your entire arm over your opponent's trapped arm, just your forearm. This will allow you to apply the proper downward pressure to garner the tap.

1

I've secured the x-guard position on Babs. Notice how he is gripping my left collar with his right hand.

2

Babs pulls on my left collar with his right hand in an attempt to nullify my x-guard sweeps.

THE X-GUARD

3

I grab the top of Babs' right wrist using my right hand. Once I have a firm hold, I break his grip and position his wrist between my neck and left shoulder. As I do this, I pull my left arm to the inside of his right leg.

4

I wrap my left forearm over the top of Babs' right elbow. Next, I grab the top of my left wrist with my right hand.

5

I extend both of my x-guard hooks into Babs' left leg and sit up. To finish the inverted armbar, I drive my left forearm down into Babs' right arm using my right hand and the strength in my left arm. Notice how I use the inside of my forearm to cut down into his elbow.

SUBMISSIONS 253

INVERTED ARMBAR (NO-GI)

In the previous technique I demonstrated how to secure an inverted armbar when your opponent latches on to your collar. In this sequence, I show you how to secure the inverted armbar when your opponent locks on to the back of your head. It is the exact same concept and the steps are similar. The only difference is how you deal with your opponent's grip.

1

I've secured the x-guard on Babs. Notice how he is pulling his weight away from my hooks.

2

In an attempt to nullify my x-guard sweeps, Babs wraps his right arm around the back of my neck and pulls his body towards me.

3

In order to be successful with the inverted armbar, I need to transition to the submission the instant Babs grabs the back of my neck. To begin, I grab his right forearm with my right hand to prevent him from pulling his arm away. Next, I pull my left arm out from underneath his right leg and begin wrapping it around his right elbow.

4

I slide my left forearm over Babs' right elbow. Notice how this turns his arm over so that his right elbow is pointing toward the ceiling. Once accomplished, I grab my left wrist with my right hand.

5

I extend both of my x-guard hooks into Babs' left leg and sit up. To finished the inverted armbar, I drive my left forearm down into his right elbow using my right hand and the strength in my left arm.

SUBMISSIONS 255

KNEE BAR

The knee bar is an excellent x-guard submission to apply on a standing opponent when he turns his body away from you and attempts to pull his trapped leg out of your grip. Although this technique can also be used against a kneeling opponent, it's more difficult because his trapped leg will be bent. When your opponent is standing, his leg is already straight, making the knee bar easy to slap on.

1

I've secured the x-guard on Babs. Notice how he is maintaining his balance on his feet.

2

In an attempt to free his right leg and escape the x-guard, Babs rotates his body in a counterclockwise direction, posts his hands on the mat, and pulls his weight away from my hooks.

THE X-GUARD

3 Maintaining my left x-guard hook, I move my right leg to the outside of Babs' right leg. Notice how I'm still controlling his right leg using both arms as I make this transition.

4 I hook my right leg over the back of Babs' right leg.

5 Still controlling Babs' right leg using both hands, I wedge my right foot under my left leg and then hook it behind my left knee. This gives me a figure-four lock on Babs' right leg.

SUBMISSIONS

6 Continuing to control Babs' right leg using both hands, I roll onto my right side. Notice how this forces Babs to fall onto his right shoulder.

7 I hook my left arm around Babs' right leg, trapping his right foot behind my left armpit.

8 To finish the knee bar submission, I drive my hips into Babs' right knee and arch backward.

GI NO-GI   THE X-GUARD

FOOT LOCK

Just like the knee bar, the foot lock comes into play when your opponent turns his body away from you and attempts to pull his leg out of your grip. With his weight no longer distributed over his trapped leg, you can move his leg to the opposite side of your head and assume the foot lock position with little effort. Before applying the submission, it is important that you get your arm low on your opponent's foot instead of up around his calf. If your arm is not in the right spot, the only thing you'll accomplish is wasting energy. Once you get this technique down, it can be very effective. I know this to be true because I used it in the Arnold Classic. In an attempt to prevent me from executing a sweep, my opponent positioned his weight back and forgot all about his legs, which allowed me to wrap up his foot and bring the match to a quick close.

1

I've secured the x-guard on Babs. Notice how he is maintaining his balance on his feet.

2

I break Babs' base and cause him to drop down to his hands by extending my hooks into his left leg.

3

I adjust my grip on Babs' right leg by placing my right hand on the outside of his knee and my left hand on the back of his calf.

SUBMISSIONS 259

THE X-GUARD

4 — To secure the ankle lock, I first need to move Babs' right leg to the opposite side of my head. I begin by lifting his right leg off the mat using both hands.

5 — I guide Babs' right leg over my head and then place his foot on the mat to the outside of my right arm.

6 — I wrap my right arm around the front of Babs' right leg.

7 — Grabbing the top of my right wrist with my left hand, I turn slightly to my left side and then pull the sharp portion of my right wrist into Babs' Achilles tendon using my left hand and the strength in my right arm.

HEEL HOOK

Although the heel hook has been outlawed in most Brazilian Jiu-Jitsu competitions, it's still legal in mixed martial arts and most submission wrestling competitions. When playing the x-guard in such tournaments, I'll often resort to the heel hook when I'm unable to underhook my opponent's leg and maneuver it over my shoulder to set up my sweeps. To assume the position I need to lock in the heel hook, I'll secure a solid figure-four lock around my opponent's ankle by overhooking his leg, stretch him out with my hooks to shatter his base, get my arms into position, and then drive him to the mat using my legs. Once accomplished, the submission is just a movement away.

1) I've secured the x-guard on Babs and established a figure-four lock on his right ankle.

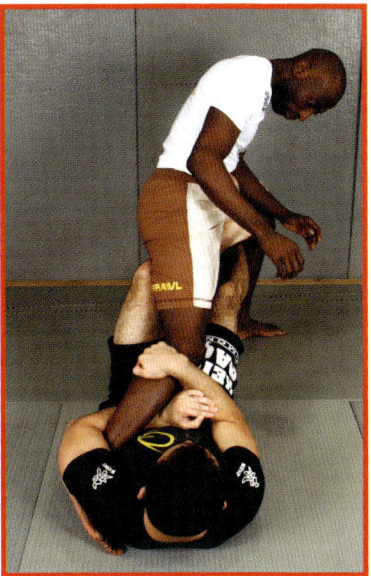

2) Extending both of my x-guard hooks into Babs' left leg, I stretch him out and topple his base.

THE X-GUARD

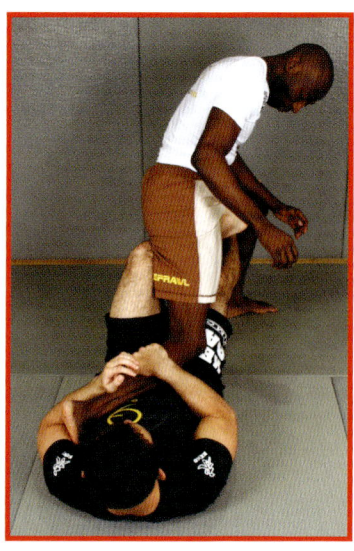

3

Pulling down on Babs' right calf with my right hand, I rotate his leg in a clockwise direction so his shin lays flush with my chest. Next, I hook the crook of my left elbow around his right heel, trapping his foot in my armpit.

4

I clasp my hands together, forming my grip just below Babs' right calf.

5

In one fluid motion, I unhook my left foot from Babs' left hip, swing my left leg around the outside of his right leg, and hook my right foot around the inside of his right thigh.

262   THE X-GUARD

THE X-GUARD

6

I place my left foot on Babs' right ribcage.

7

I force Babs to the mat by driving my left foot into his right ribcage.

8

Now that I forced Babs to the mat, I finish the heel hook by rotating slightly to my left and driving his right heel upwards using my arms.

SUBMISSIONS 263

MARCELO GARCIA is a five-time Brazilian Jiu-Jitsu World Champion and a three-time ADCC Submission Wrestling World Champion. He has competed and taught jiu-jitsu all over the world.

ERICH KRAUSS is a professional Muay Thai kickboxer who has lived and fought in Thailand. He has written for the New York Times and is the author of eighteen books. His first fiction title will be released in 2008.

GLEN CORDOZA is a professional Muay Thai kickboxer and mixed martial arts fighter. He is the author of six books on the martial arts.

ERIC HENDRIKX is a professional action sports photographer who has worked with the likes of Eddie Bravo and Randy Couture. He trains jiu-jitsu in San Diego, California.